THE PICTURE BOOK OF

CAVES

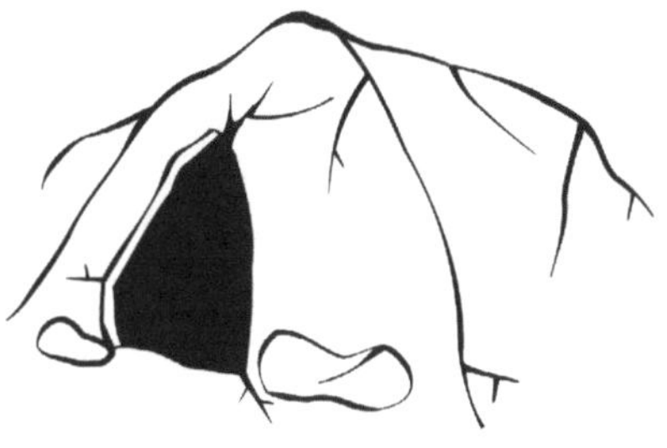

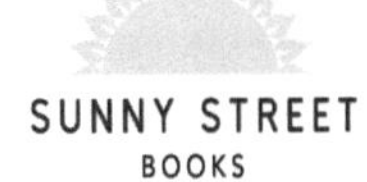

SUNNY STREET
BOOKS

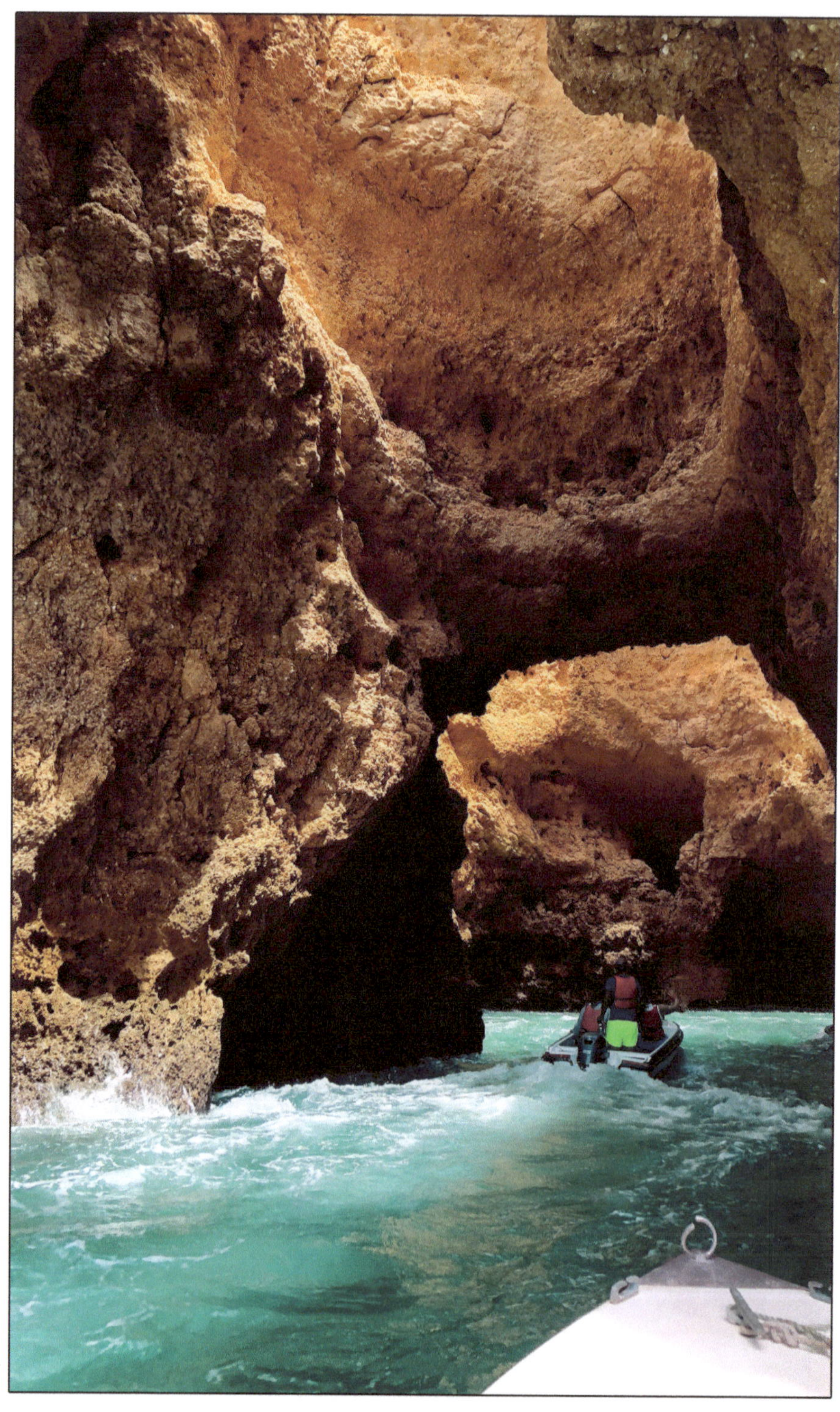

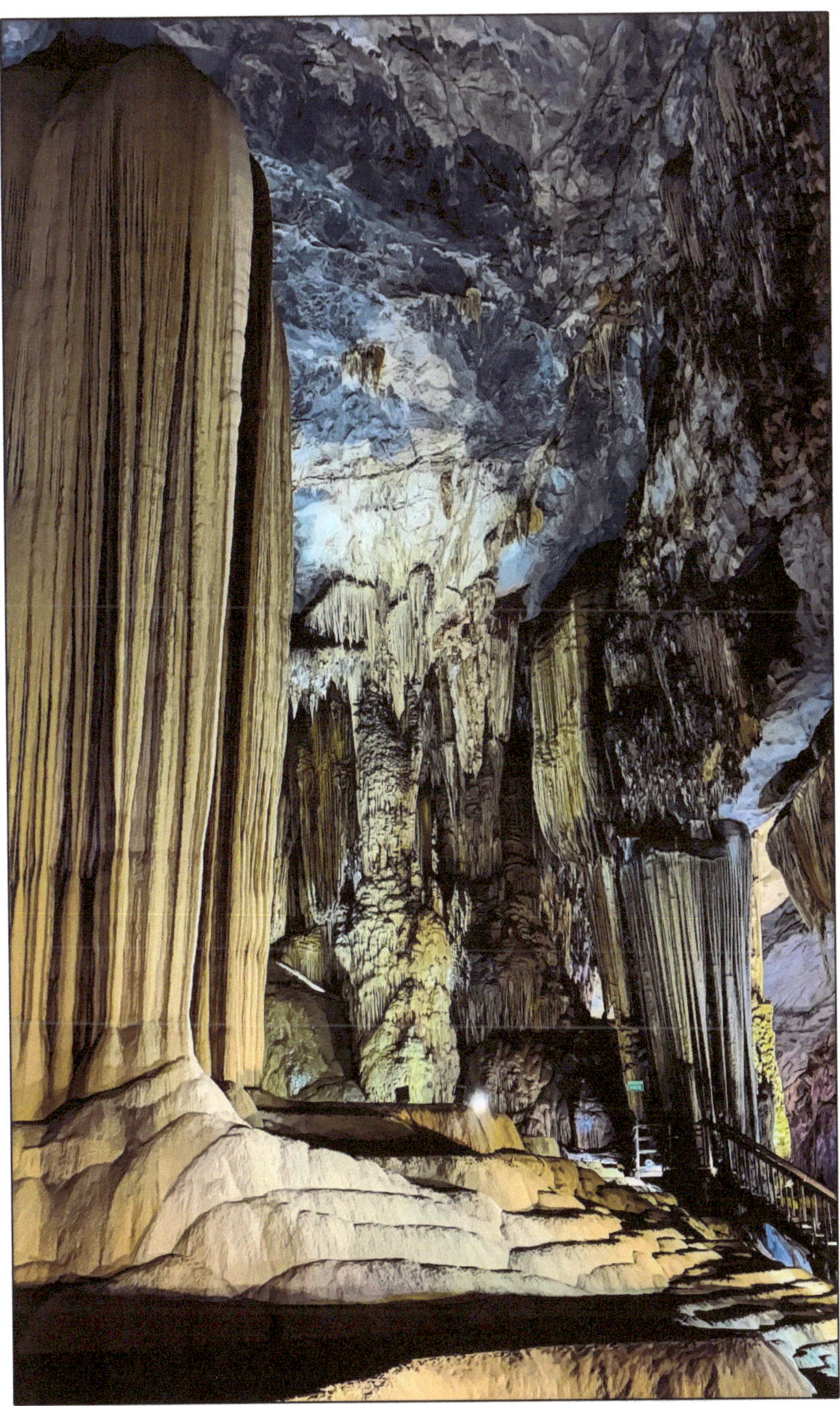

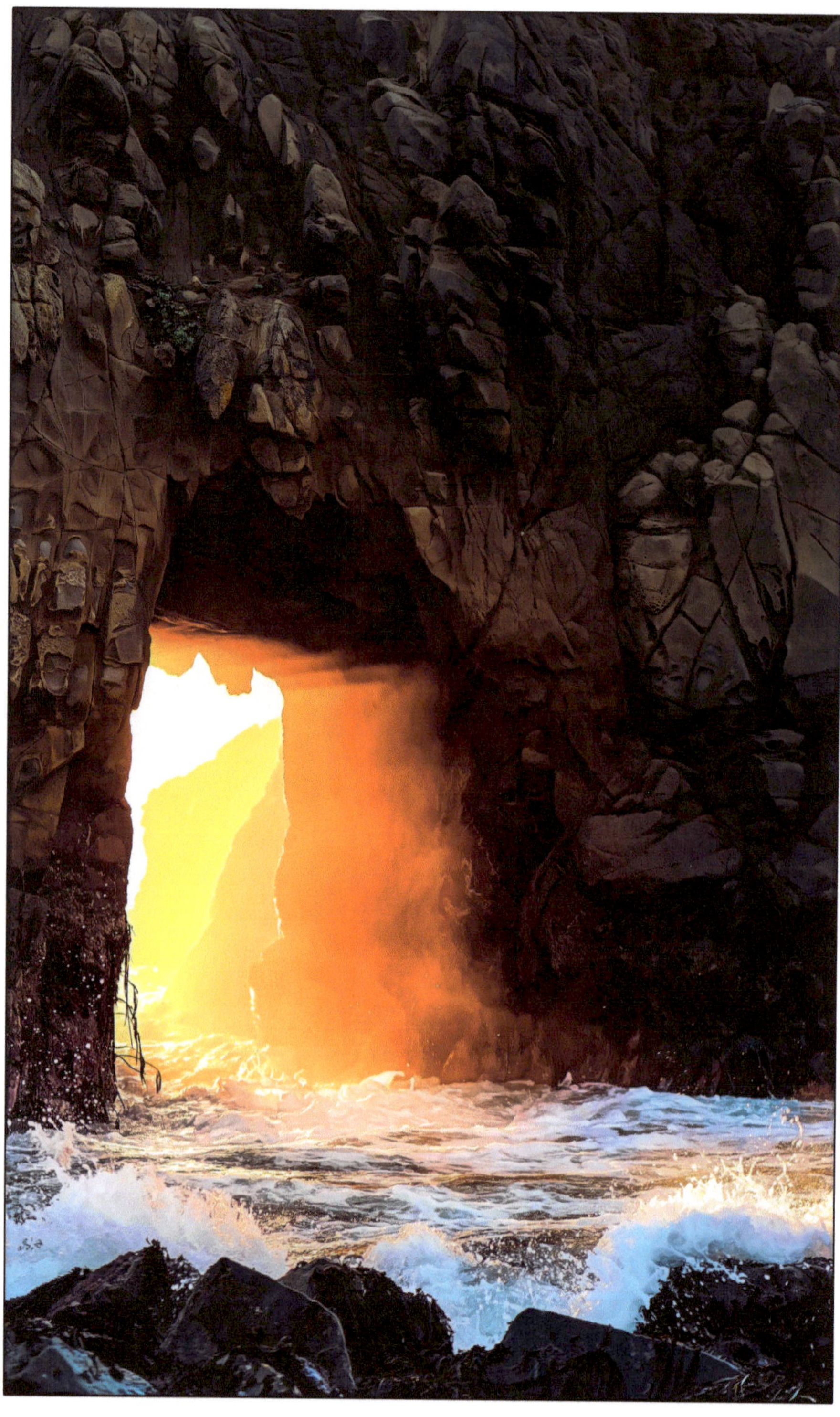

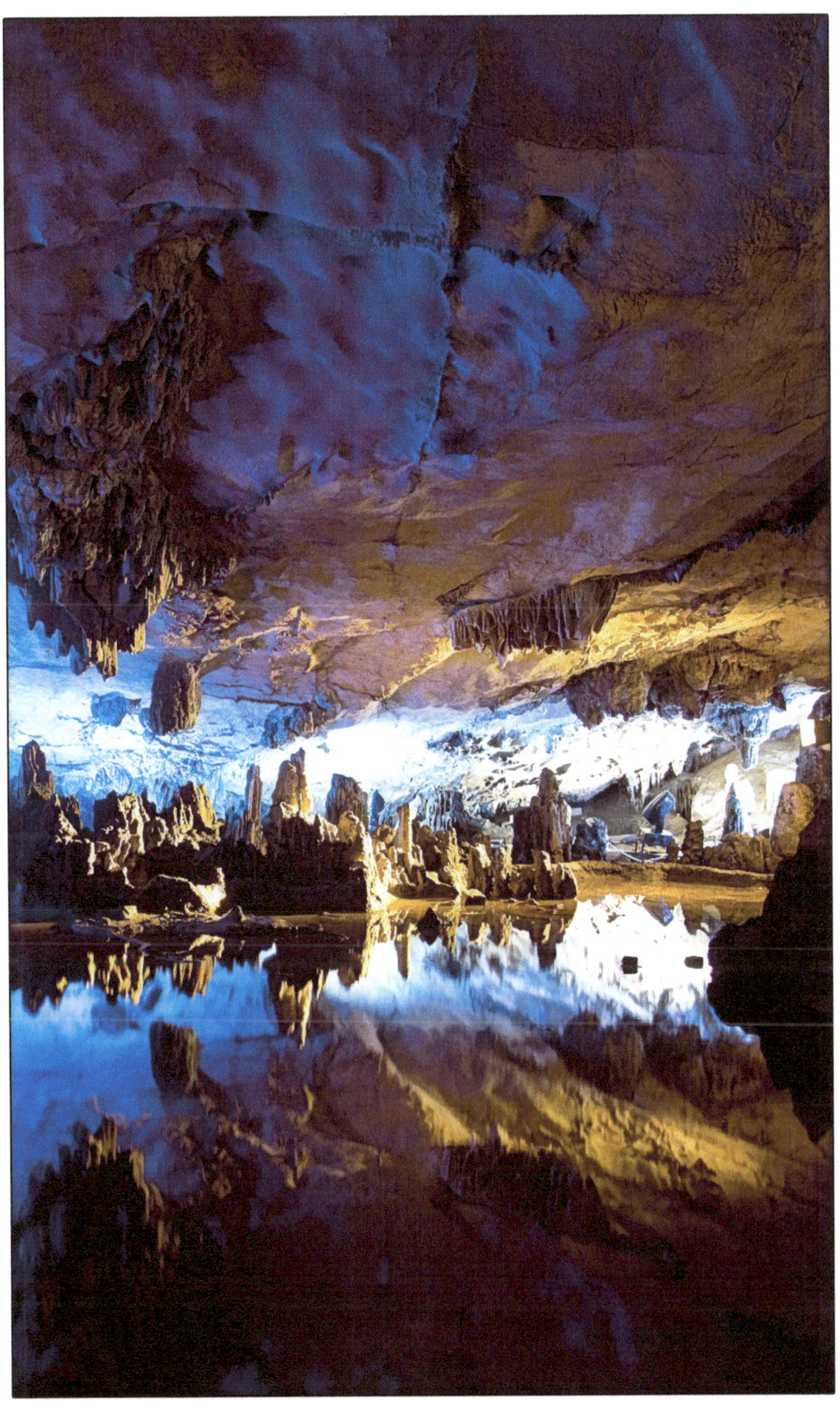

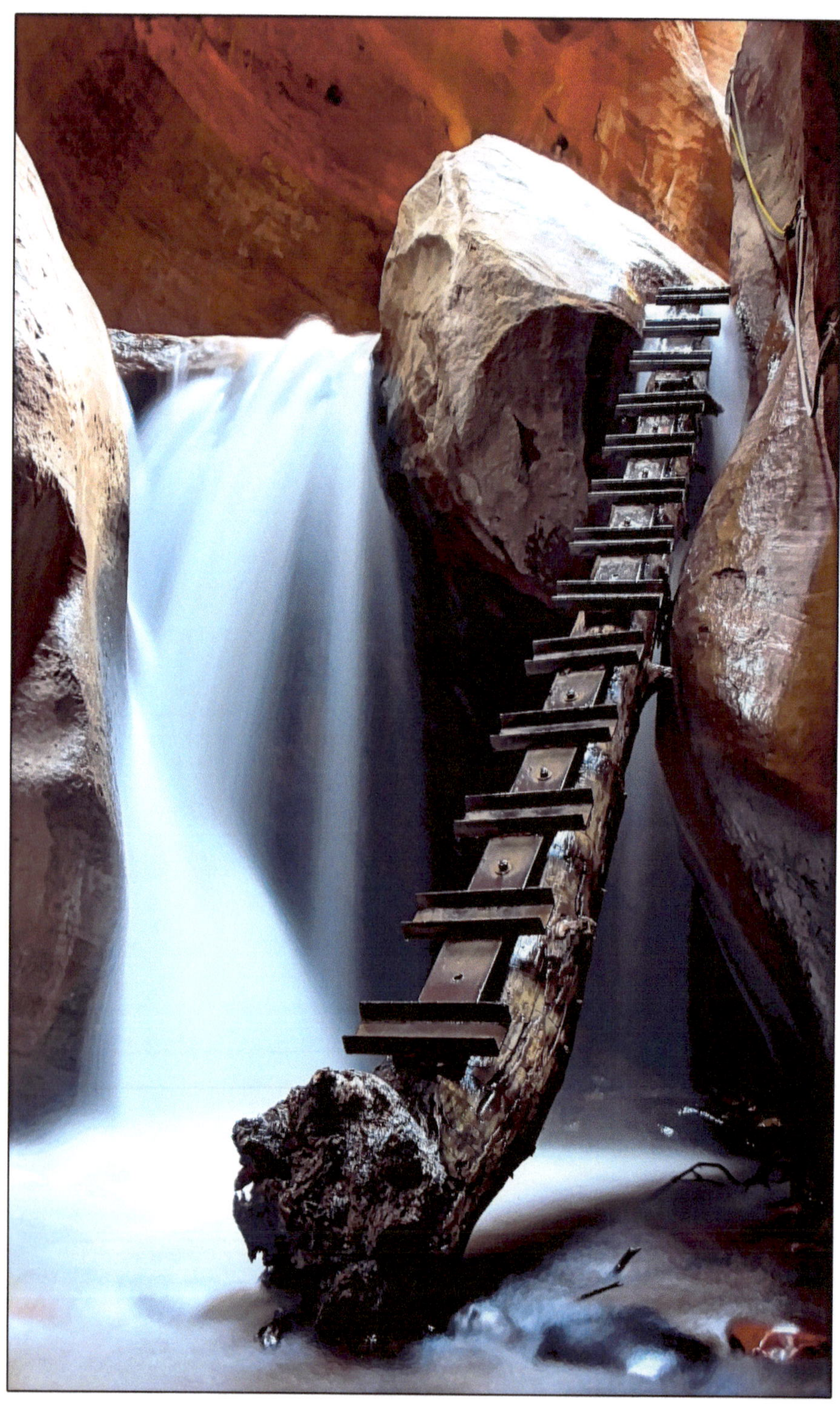

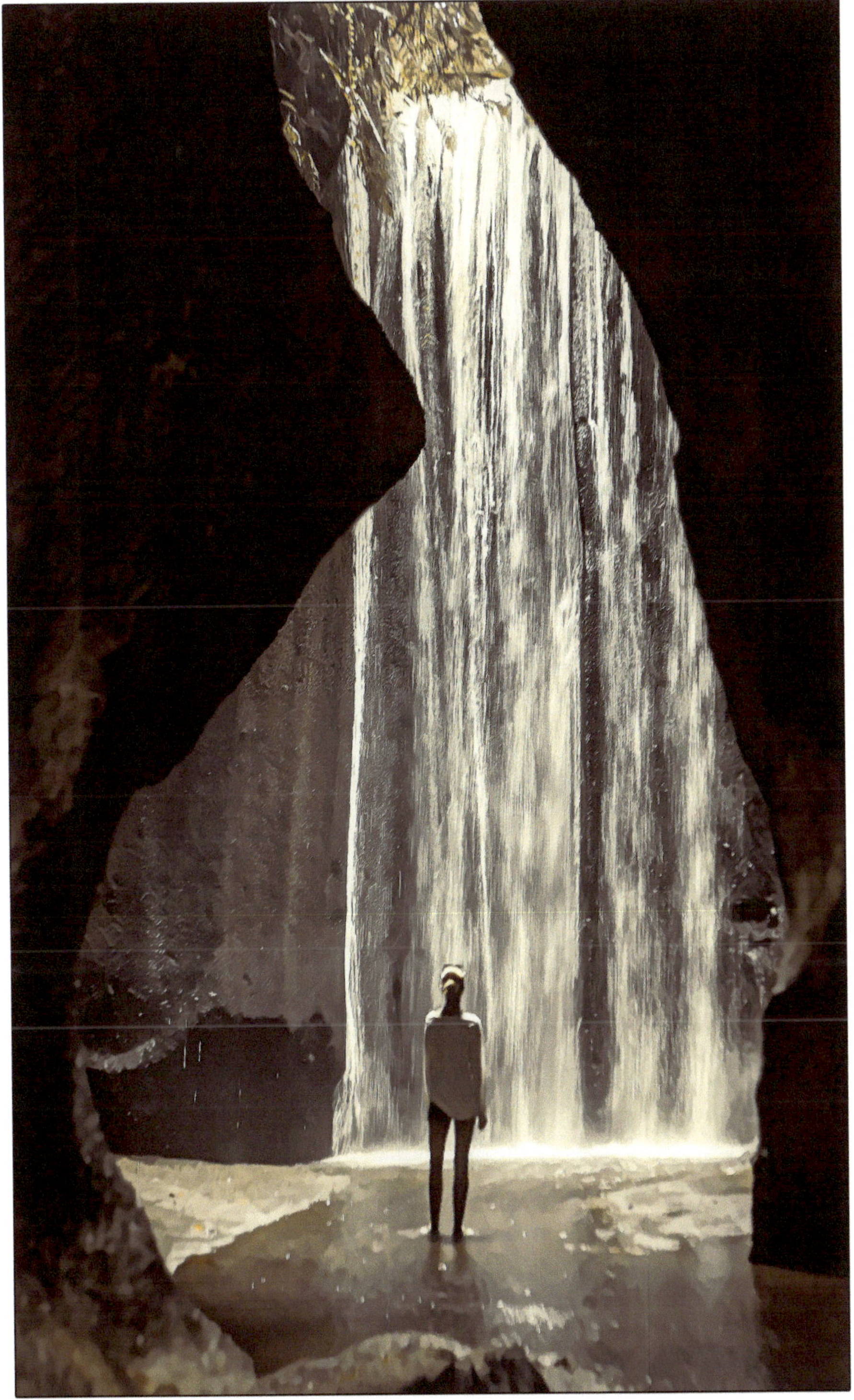

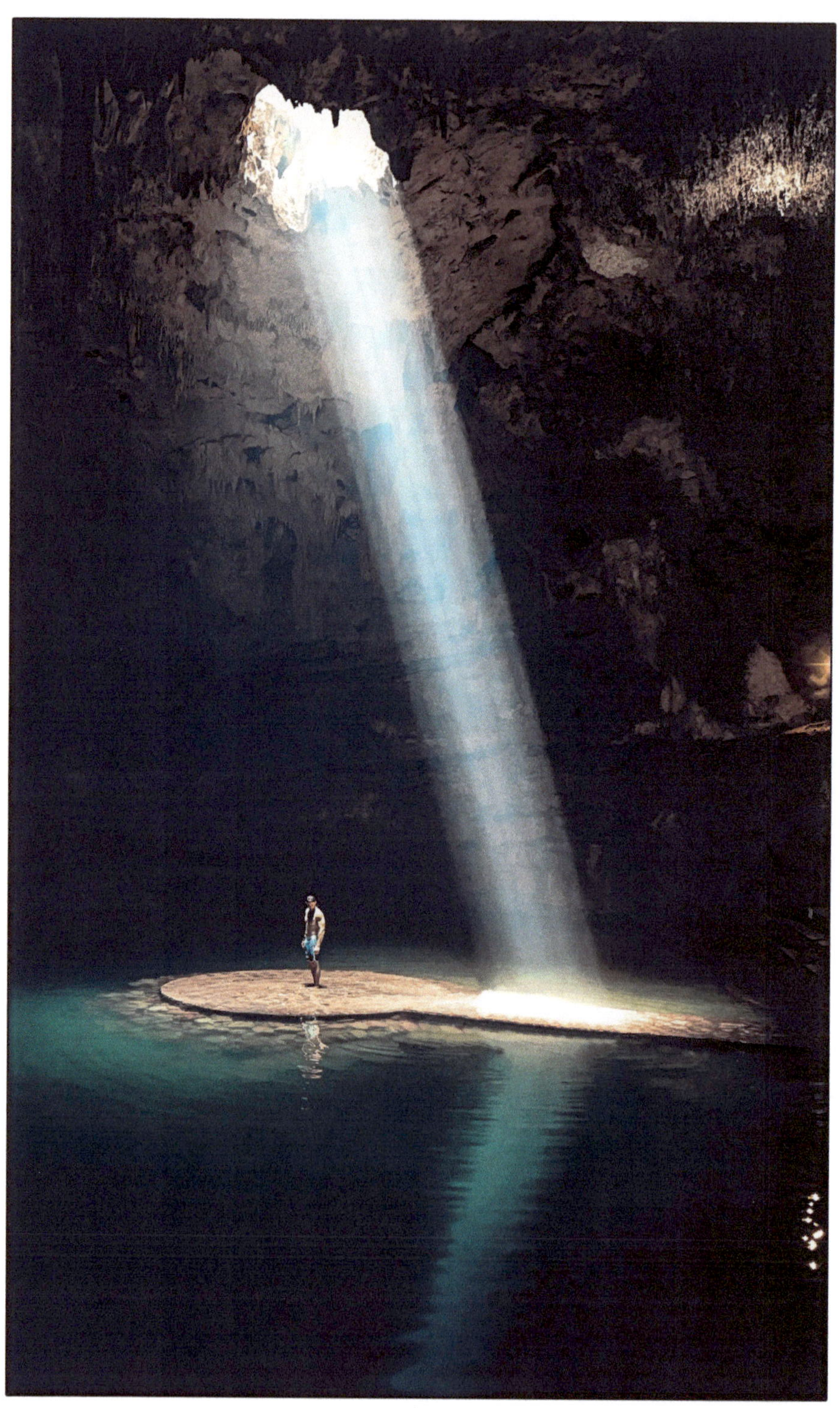

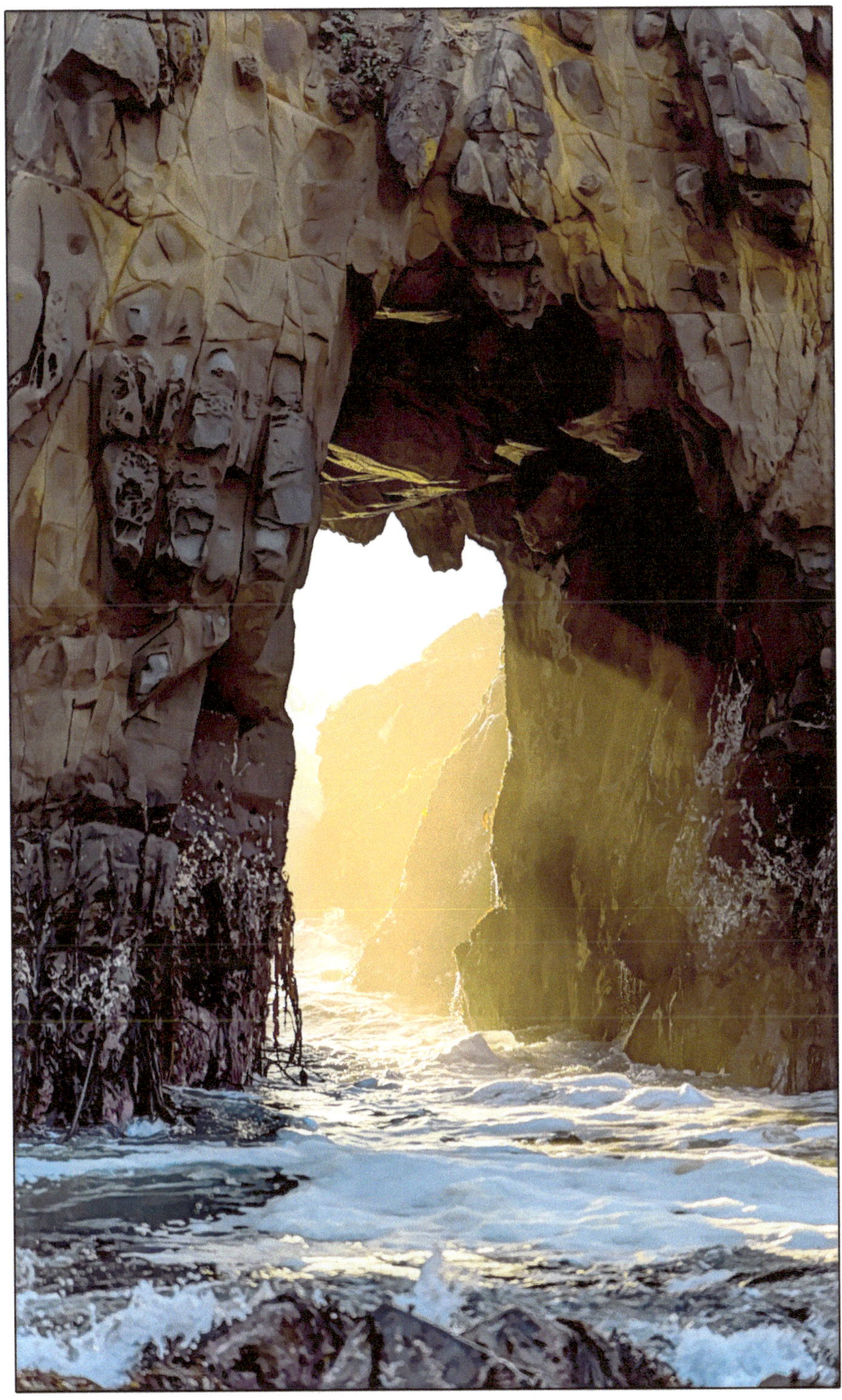

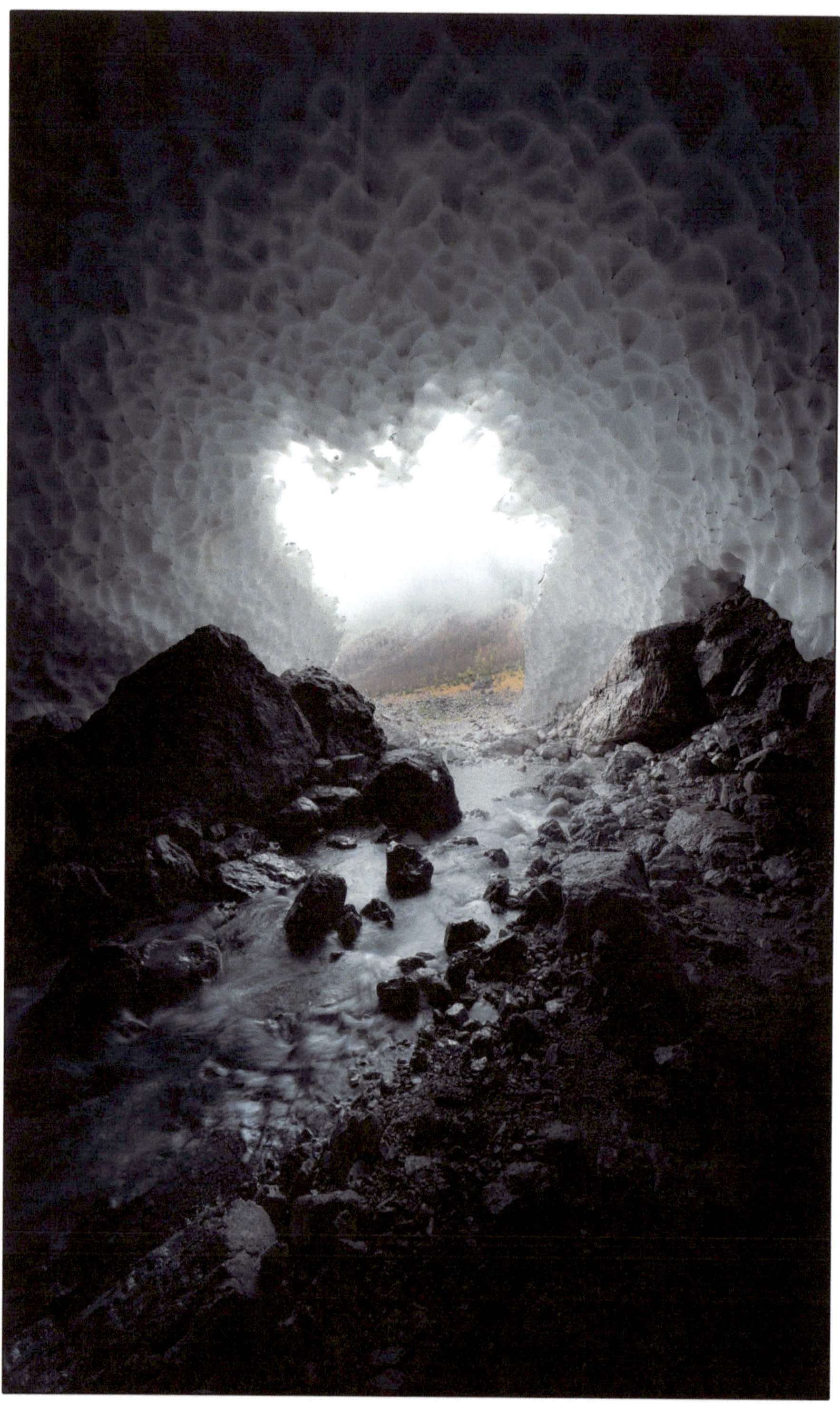

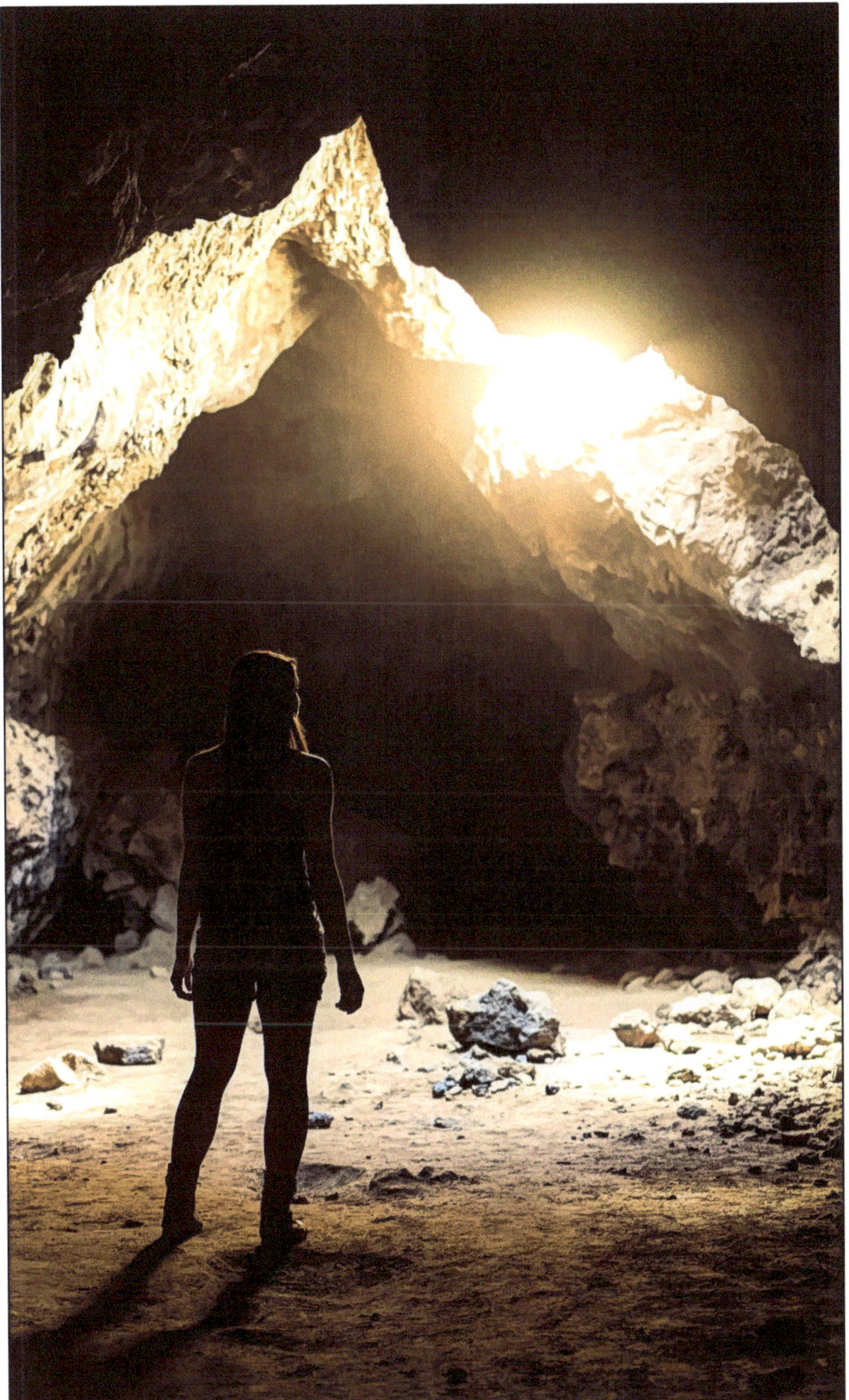

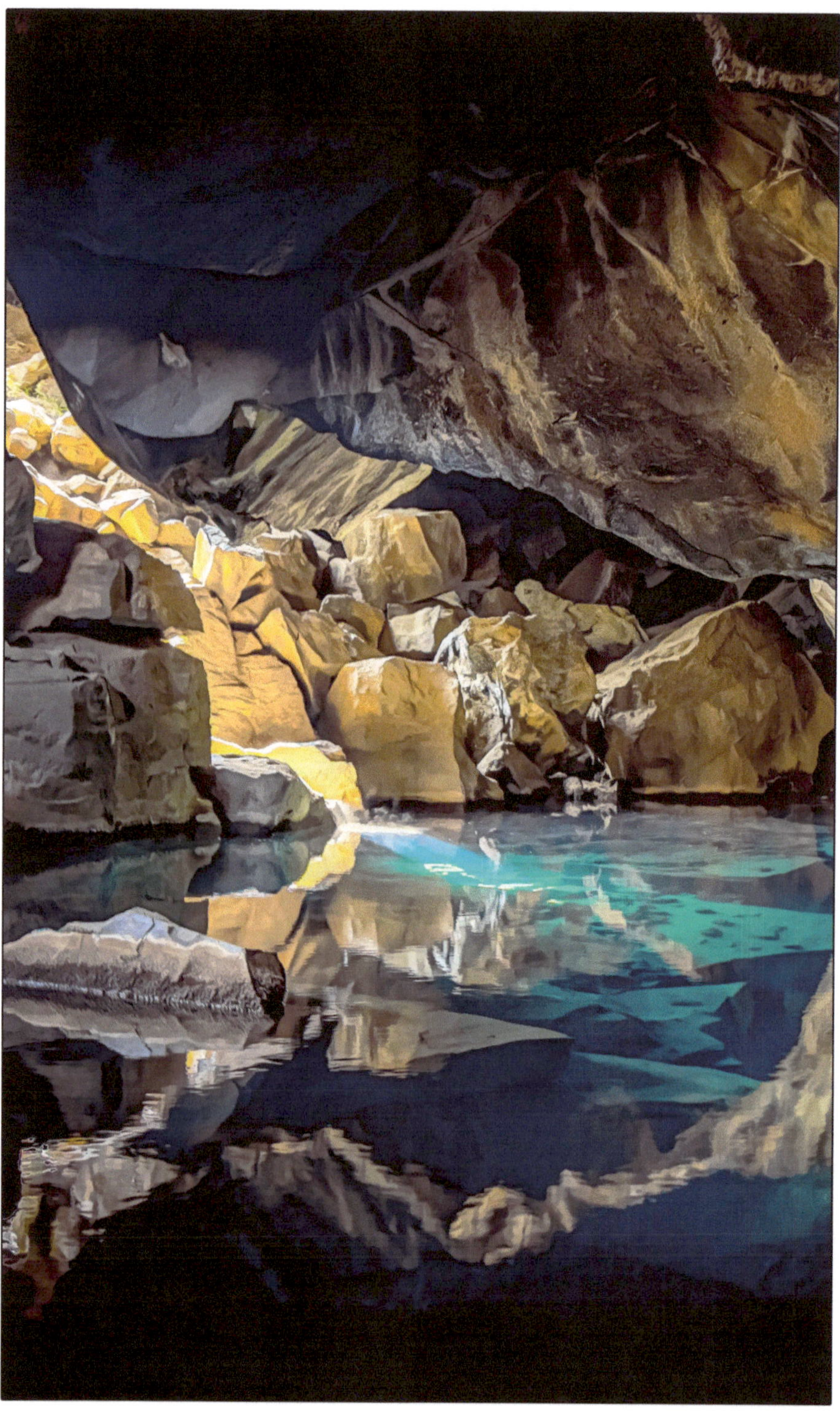

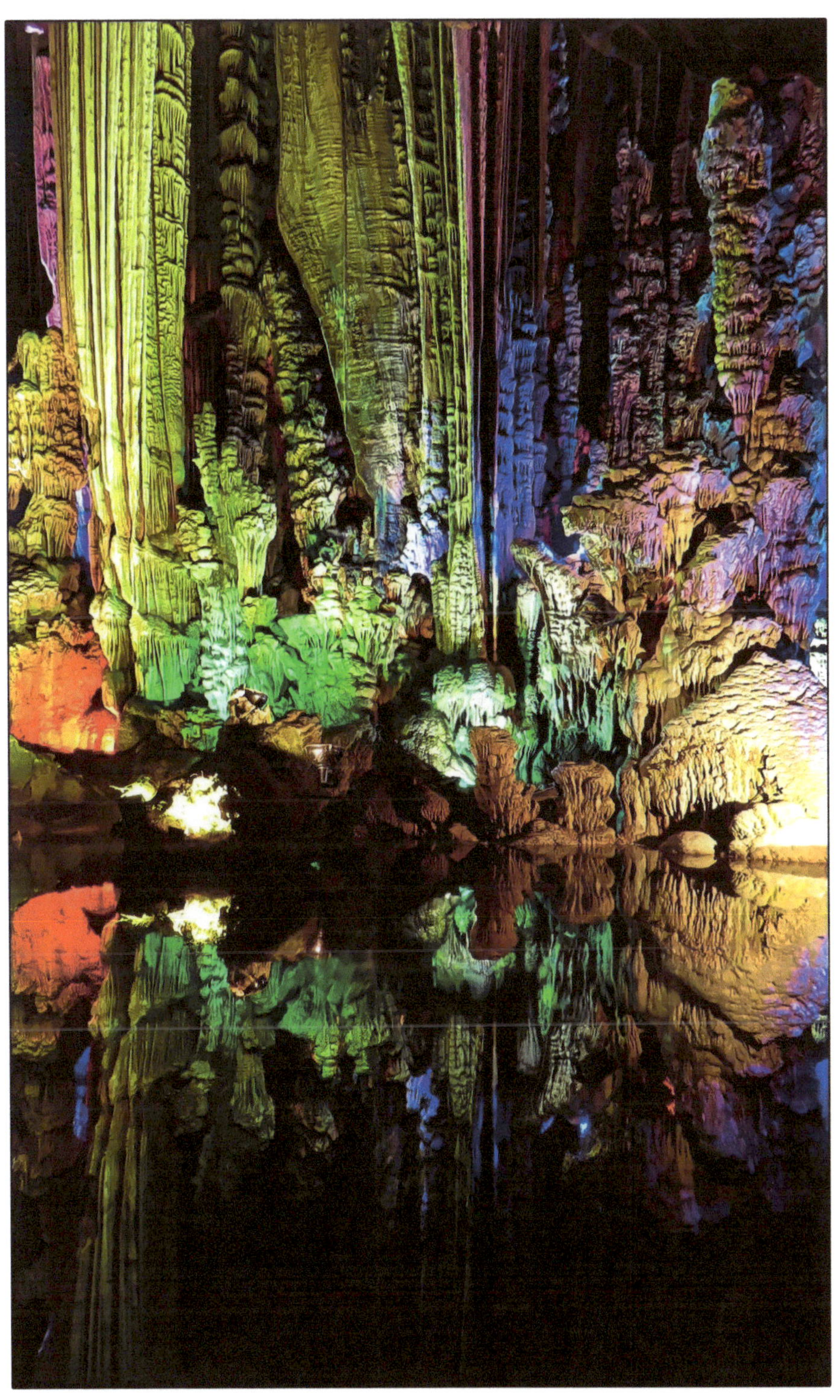

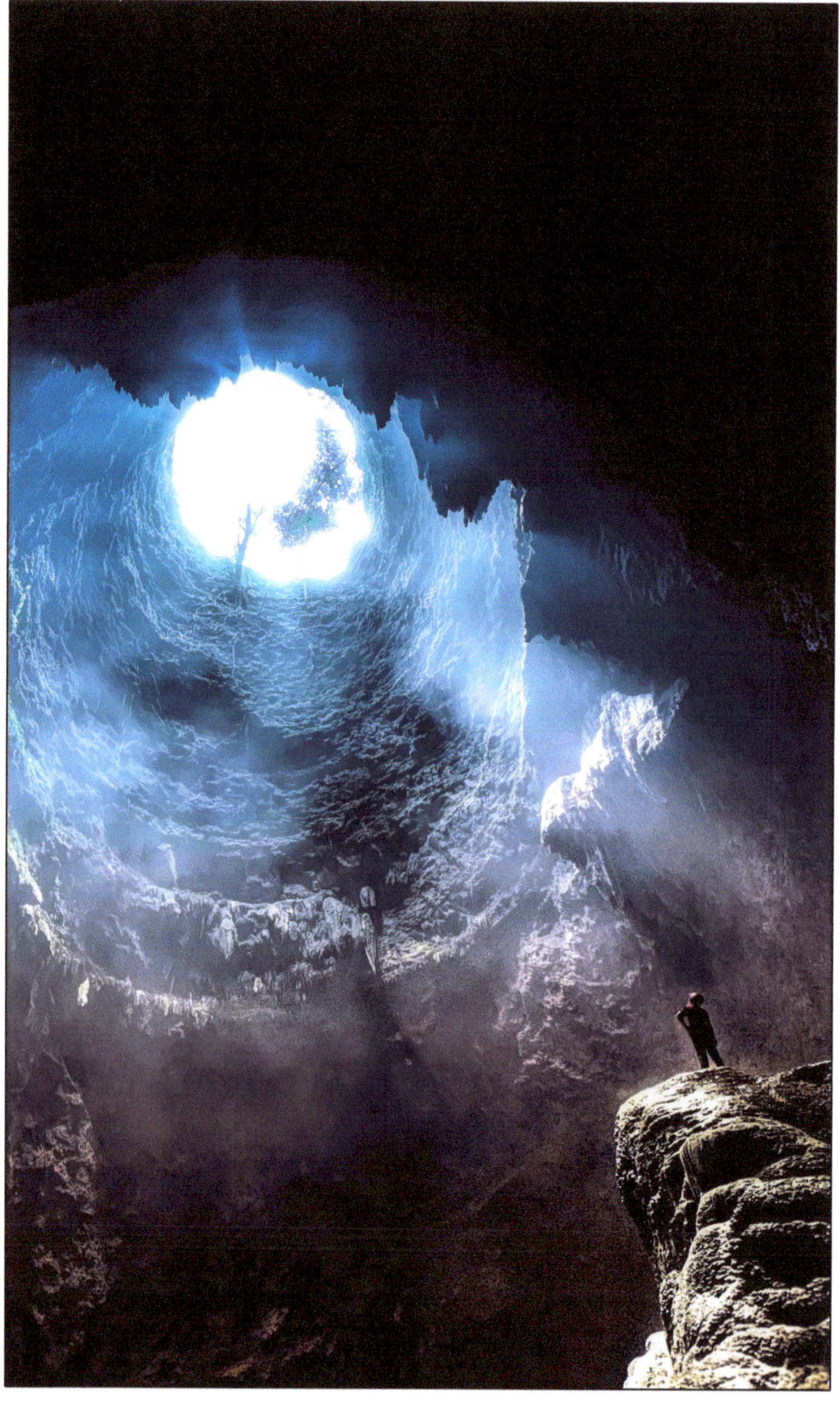

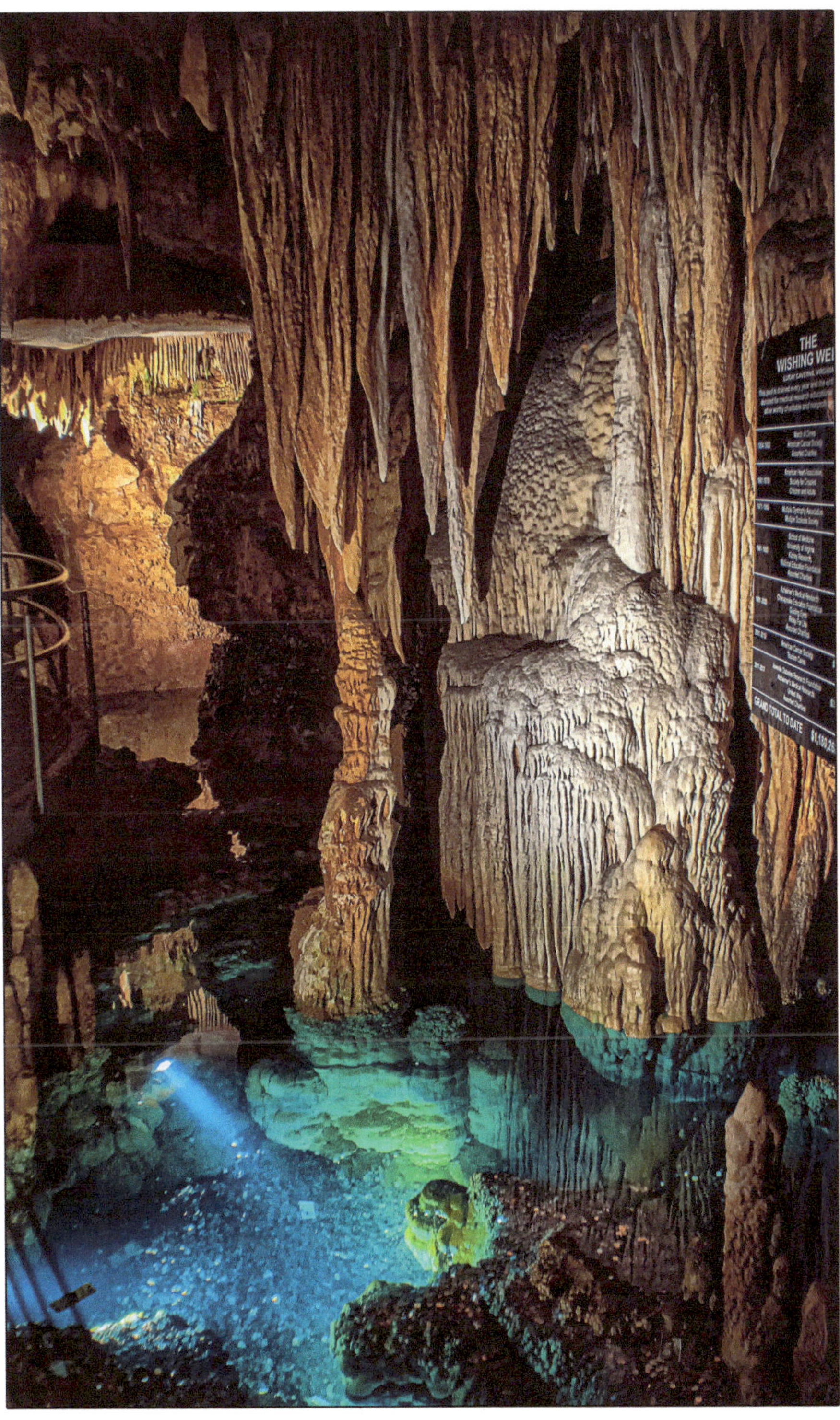

THE
WISHING WELL
GRAND TOTAL TO DATE

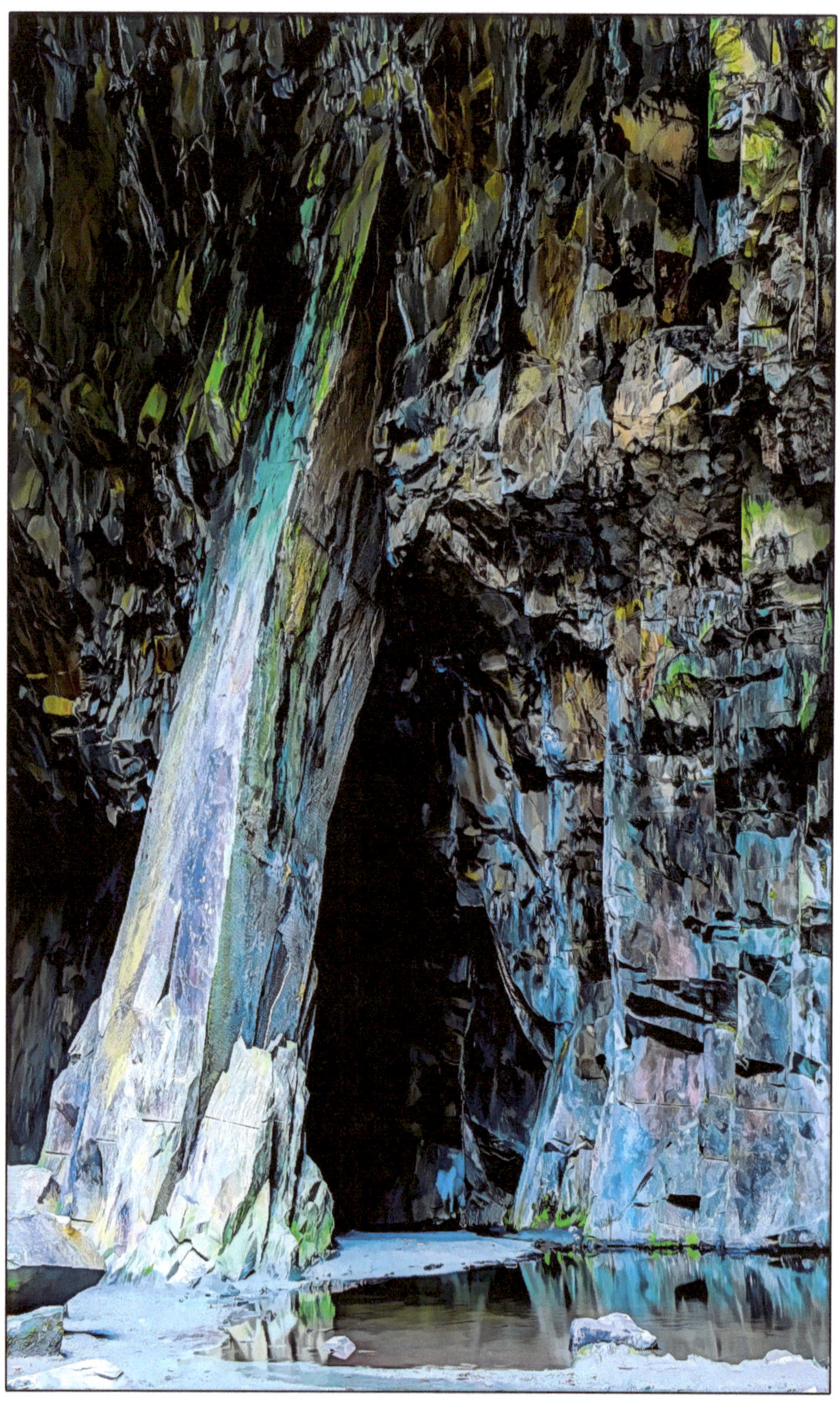

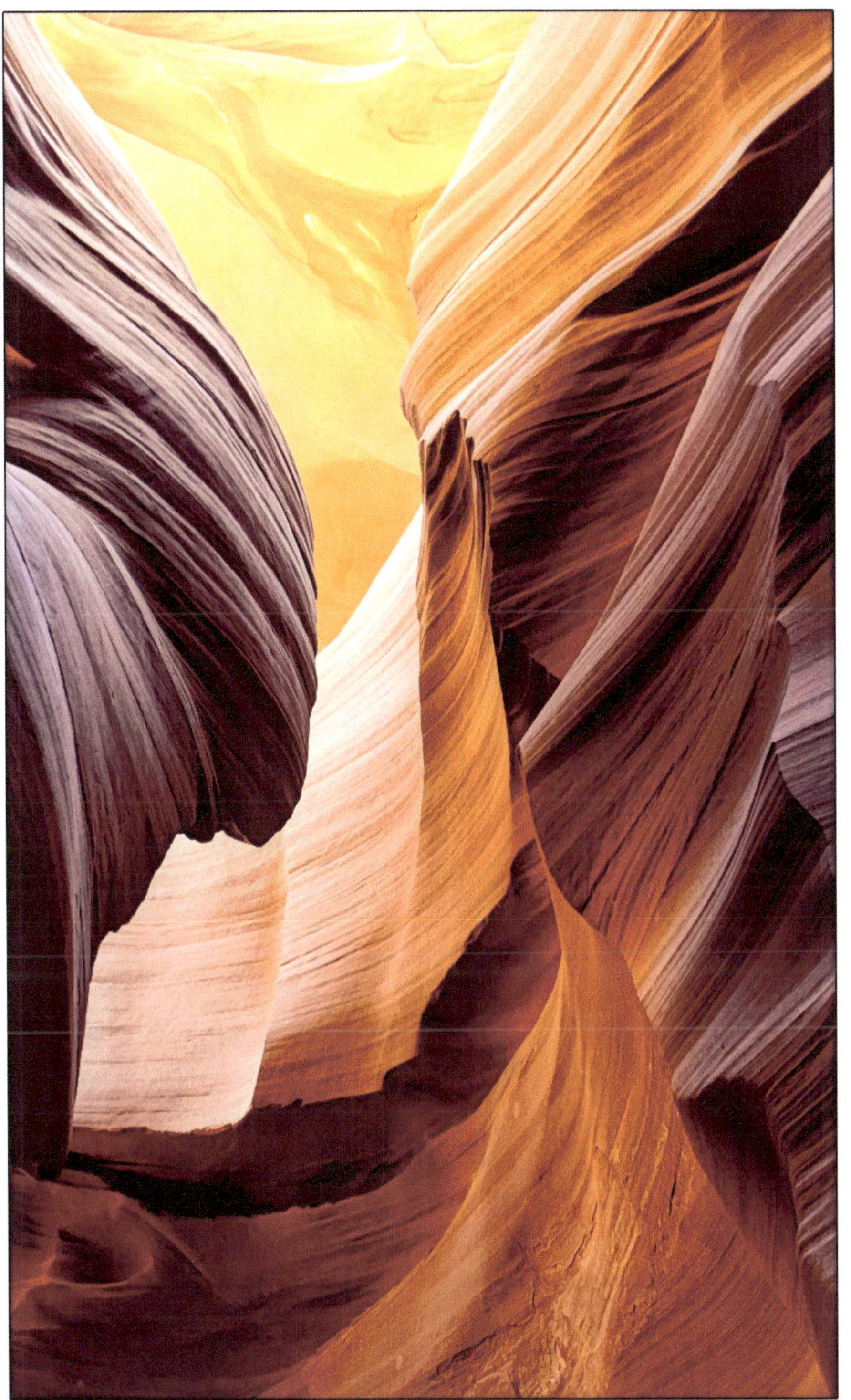

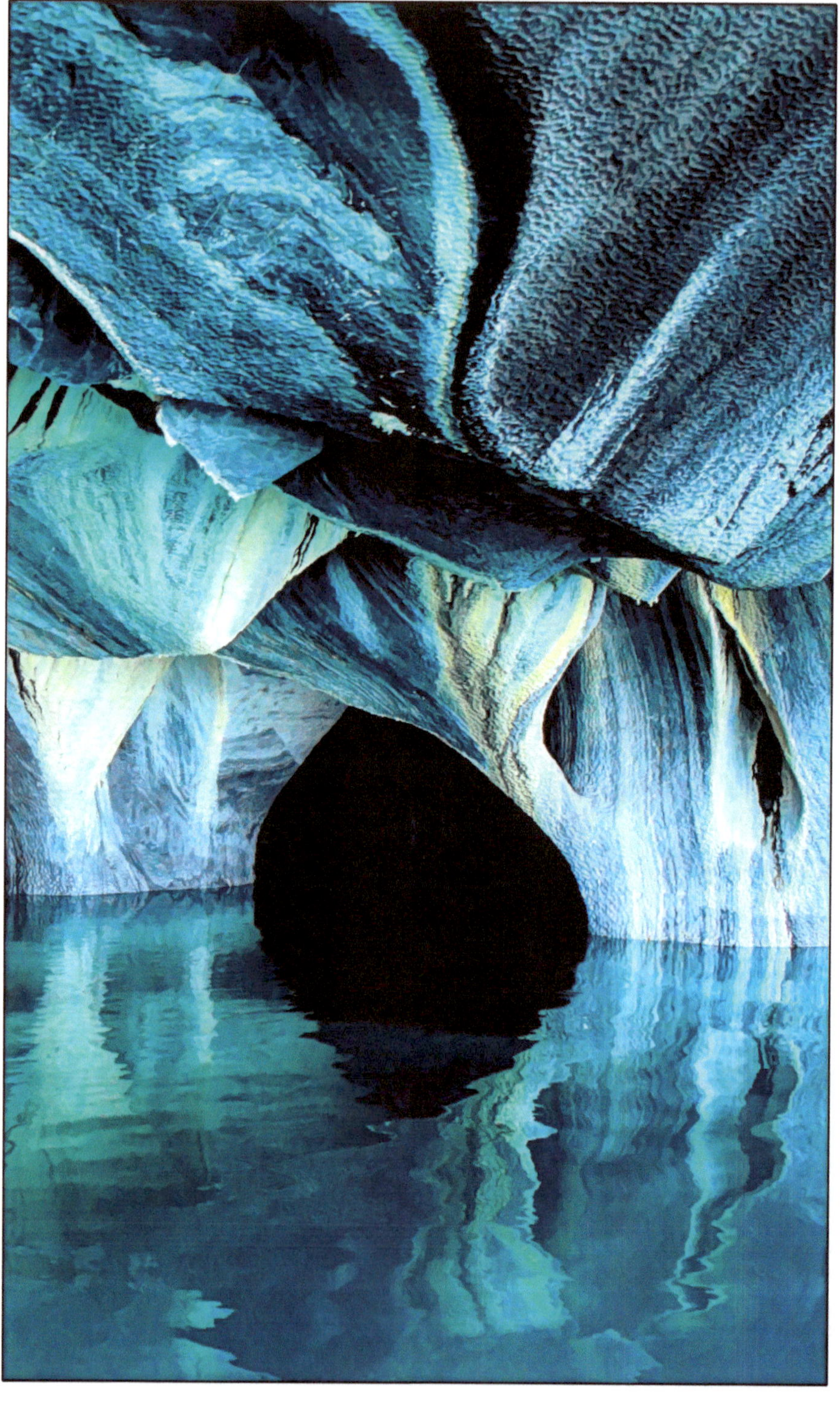

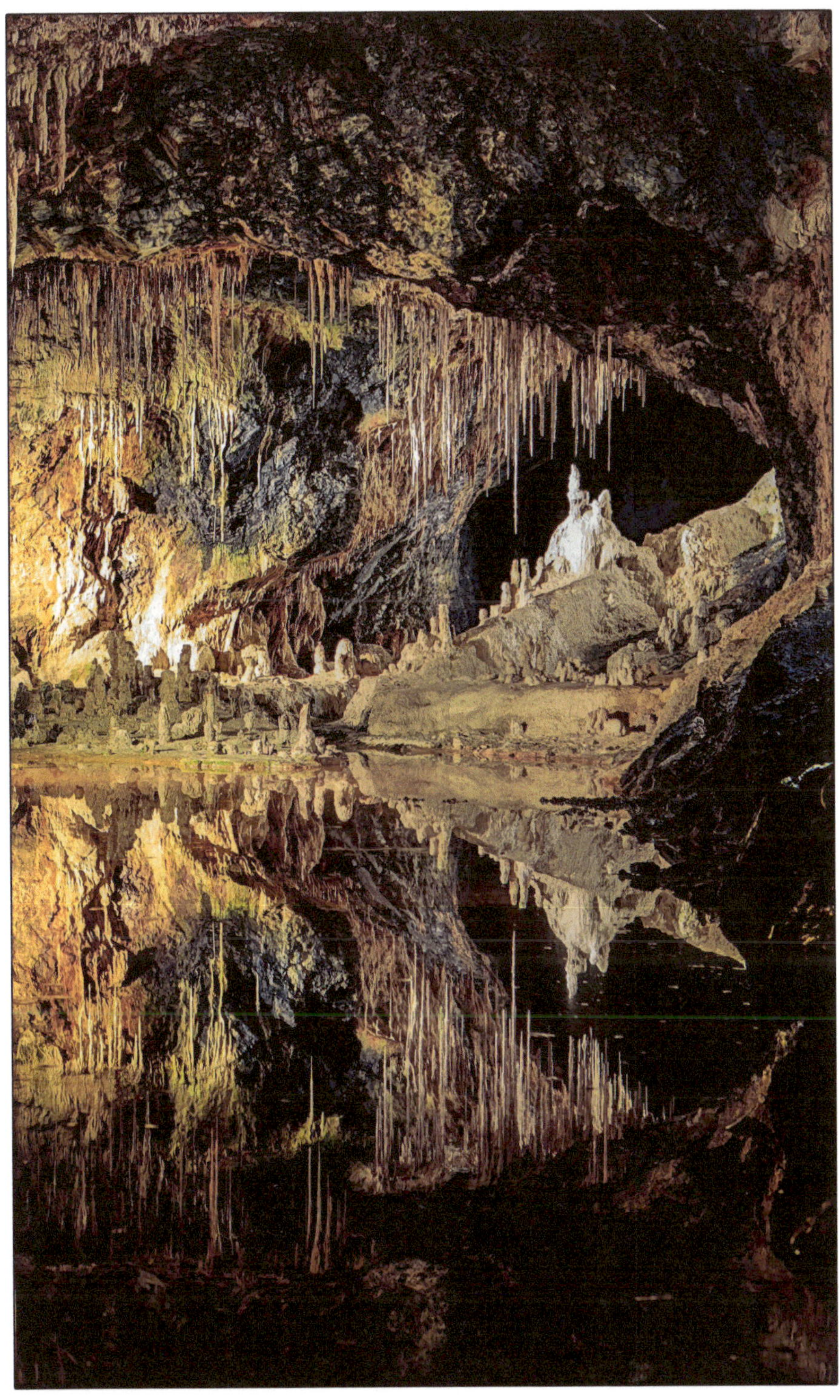

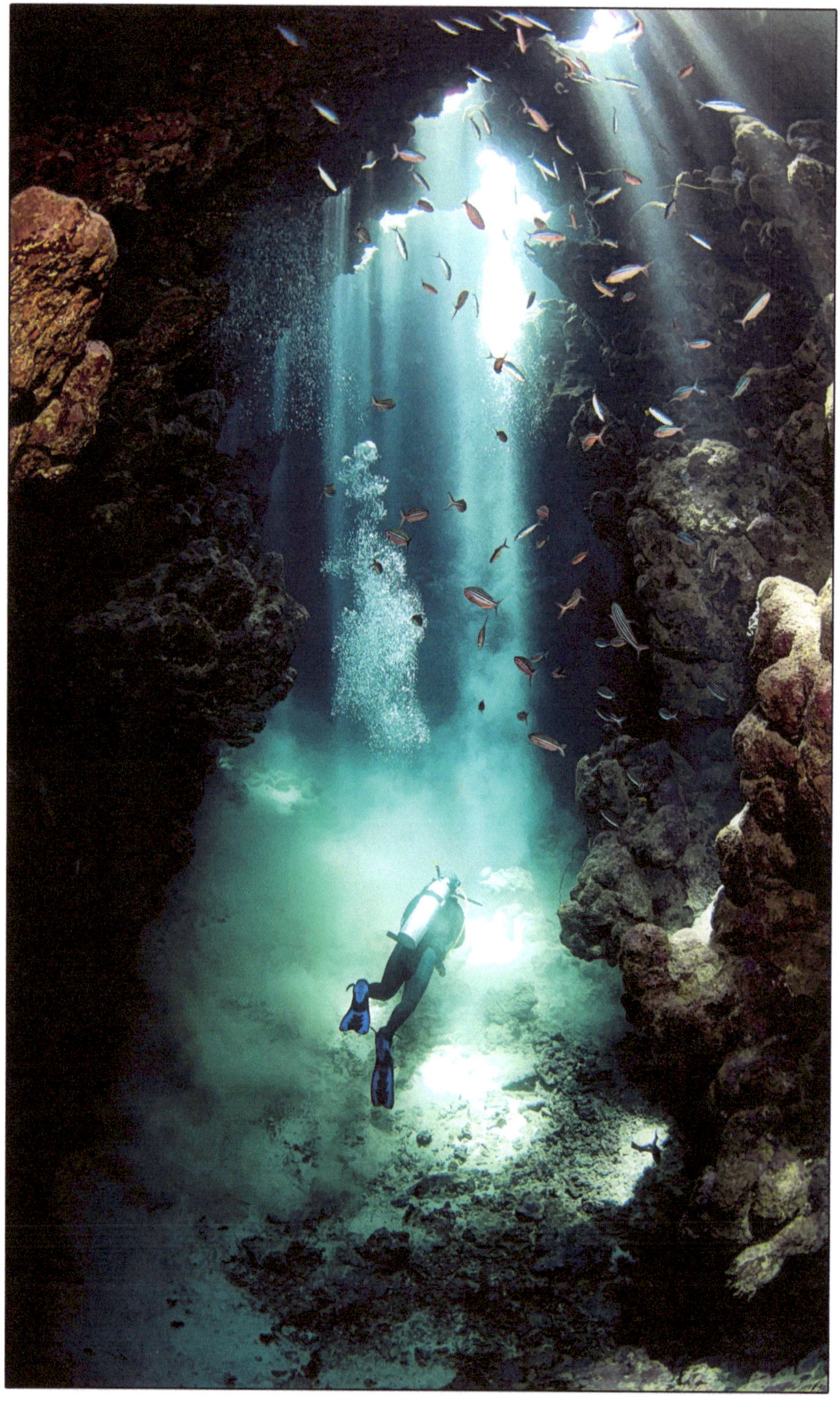

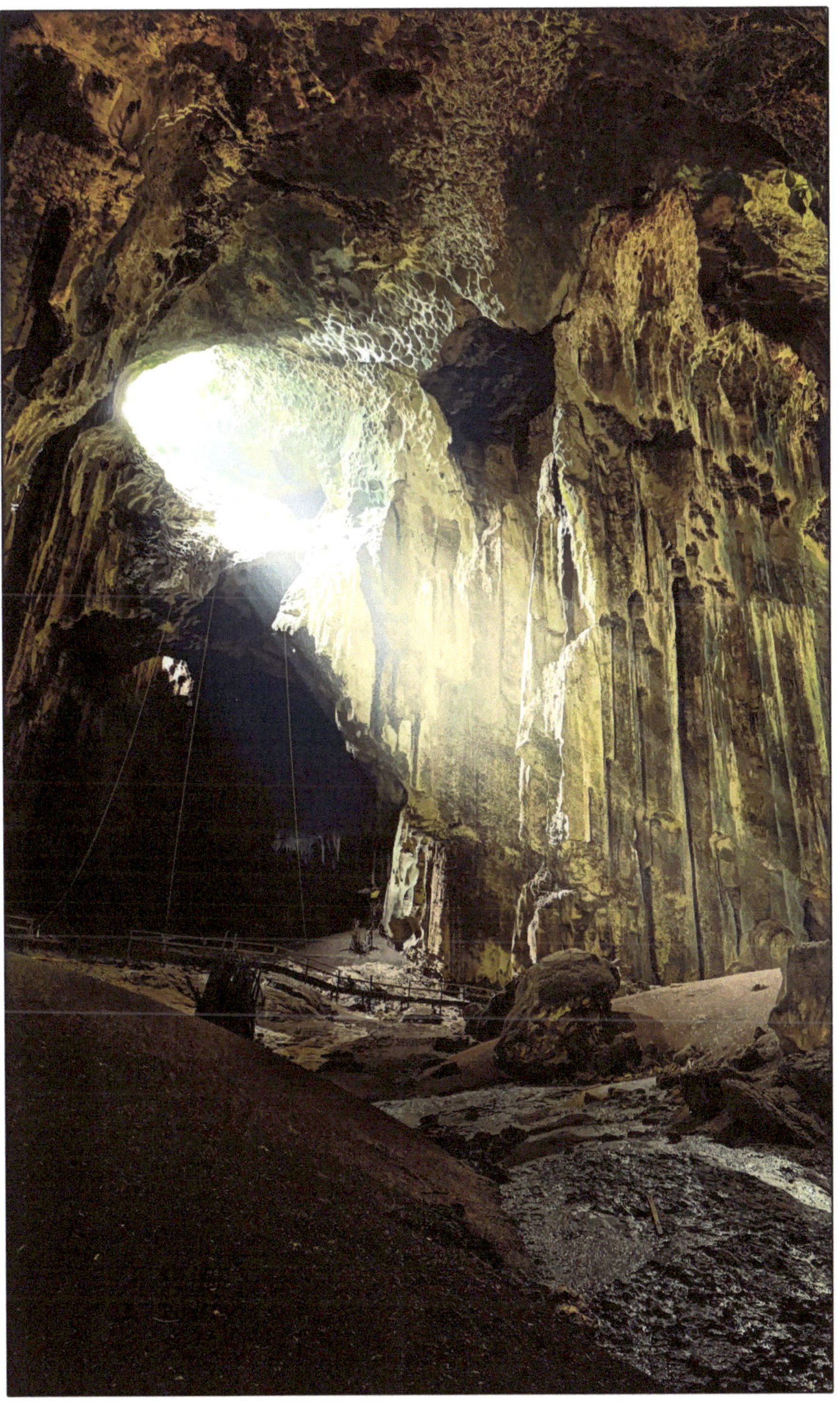

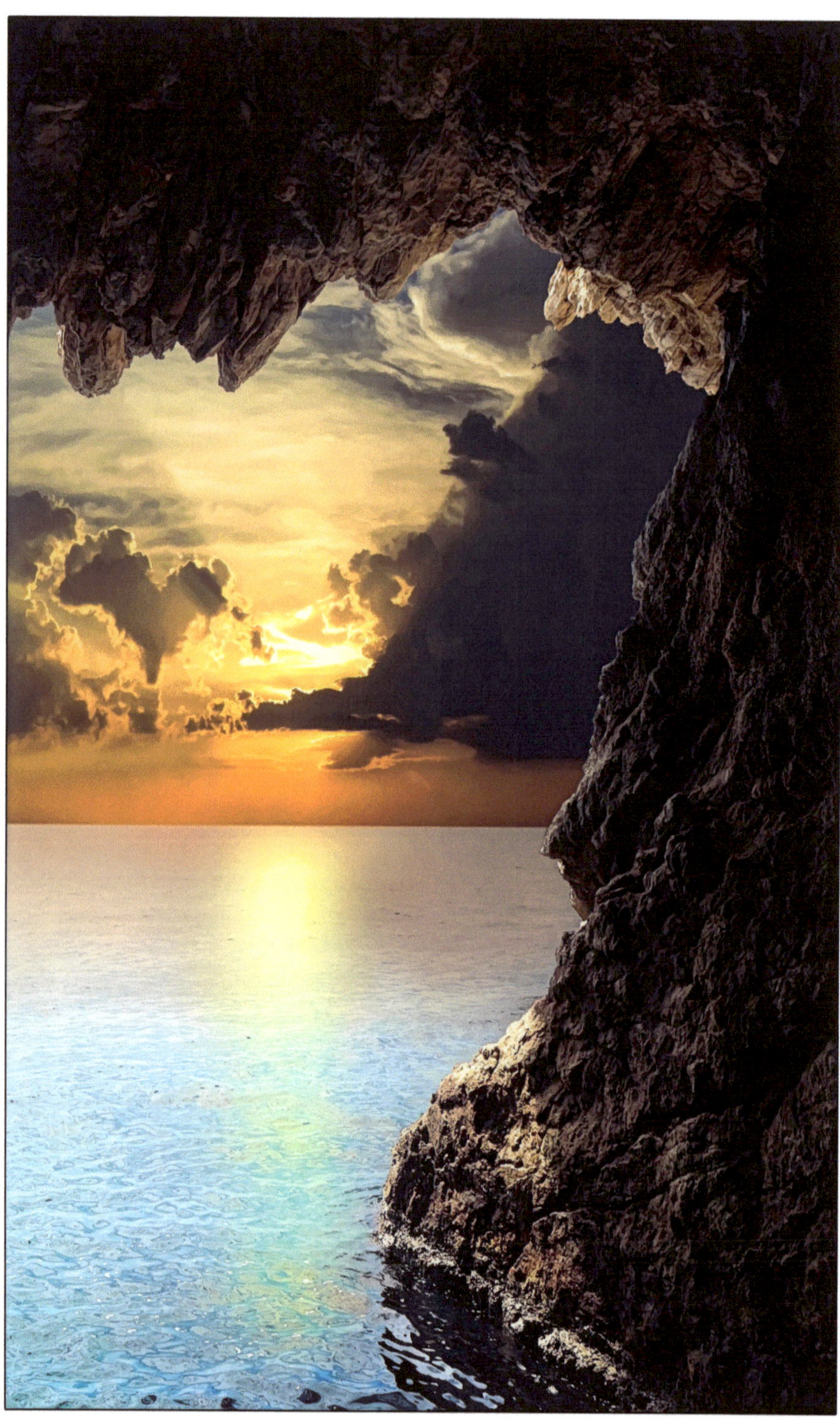

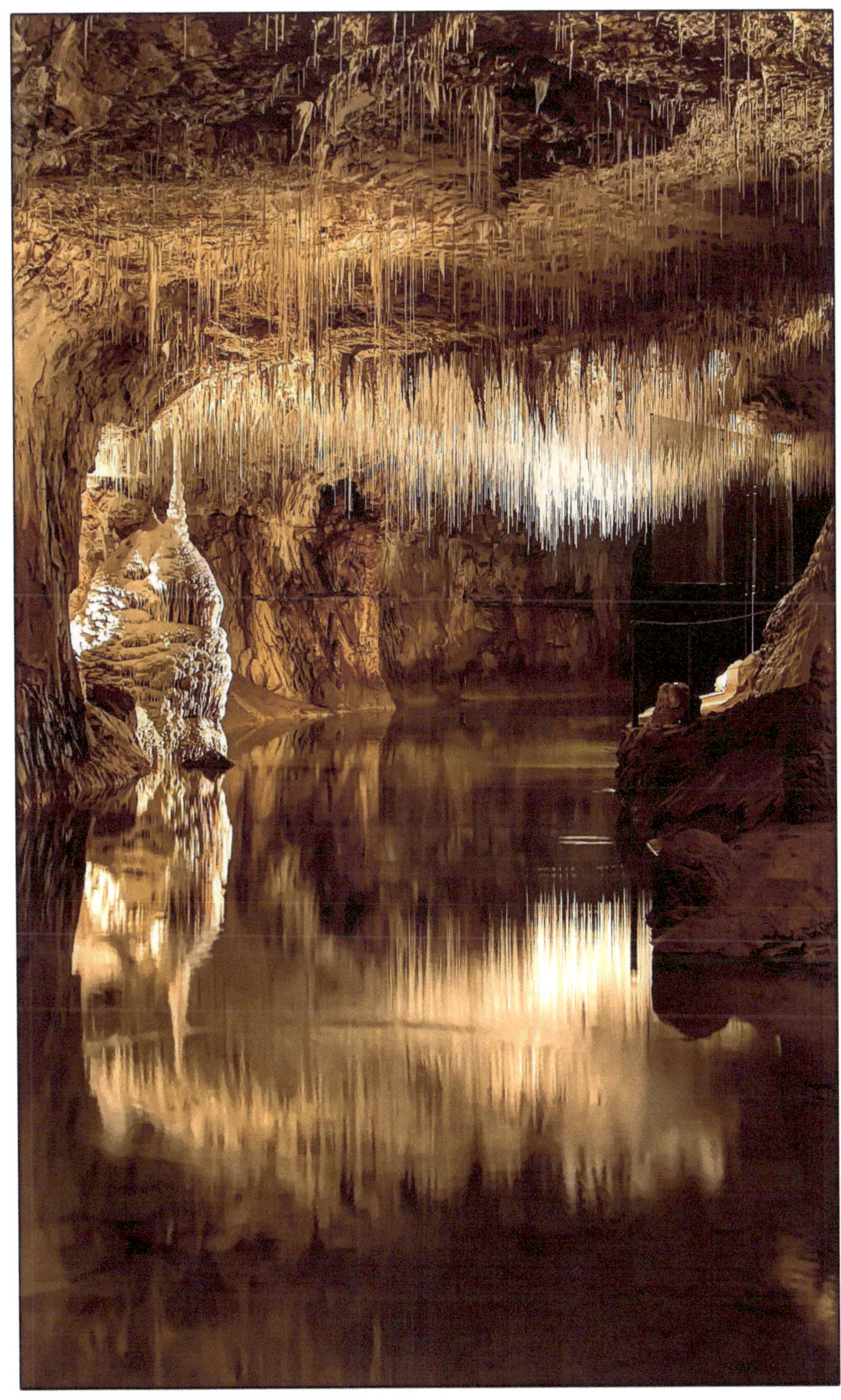

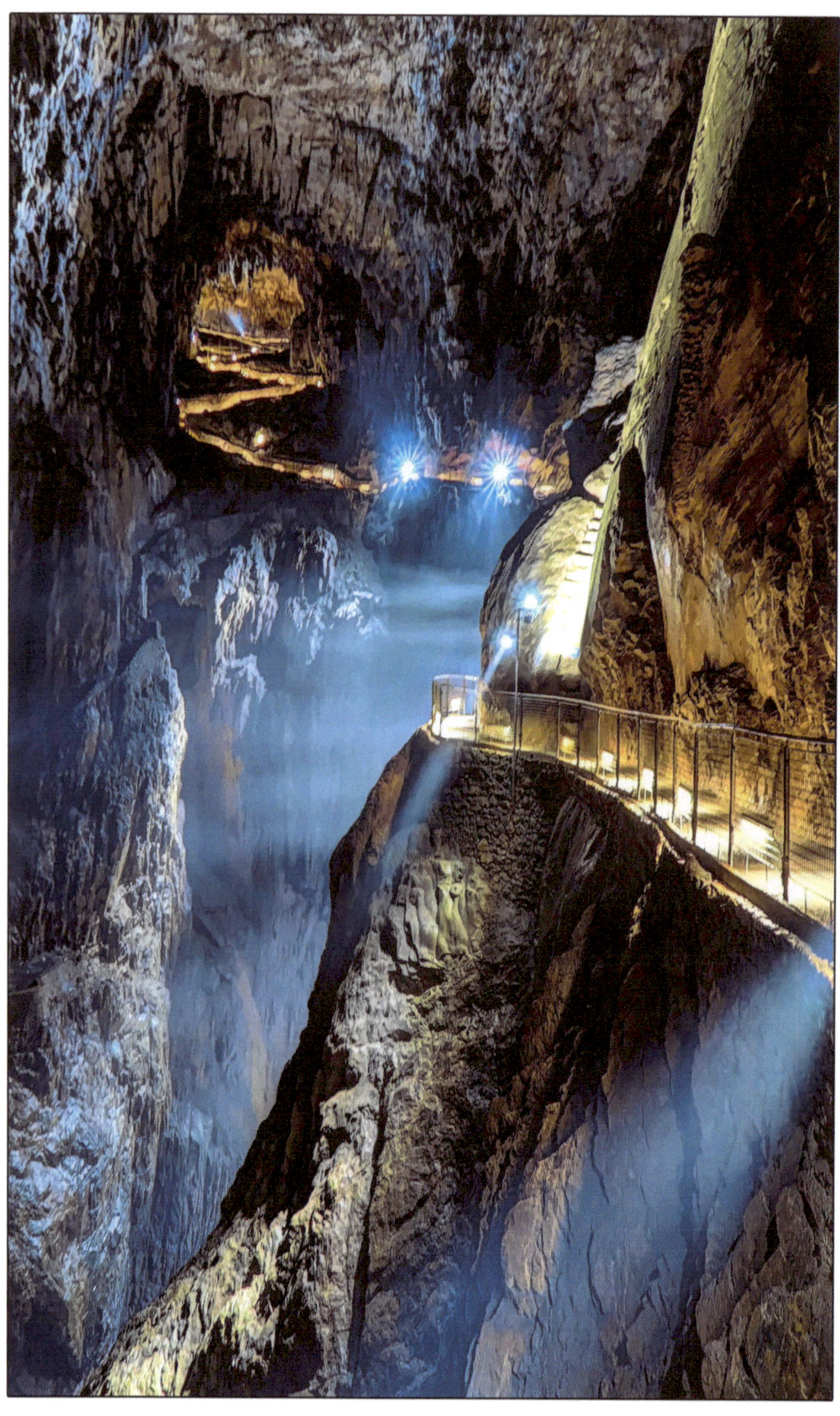

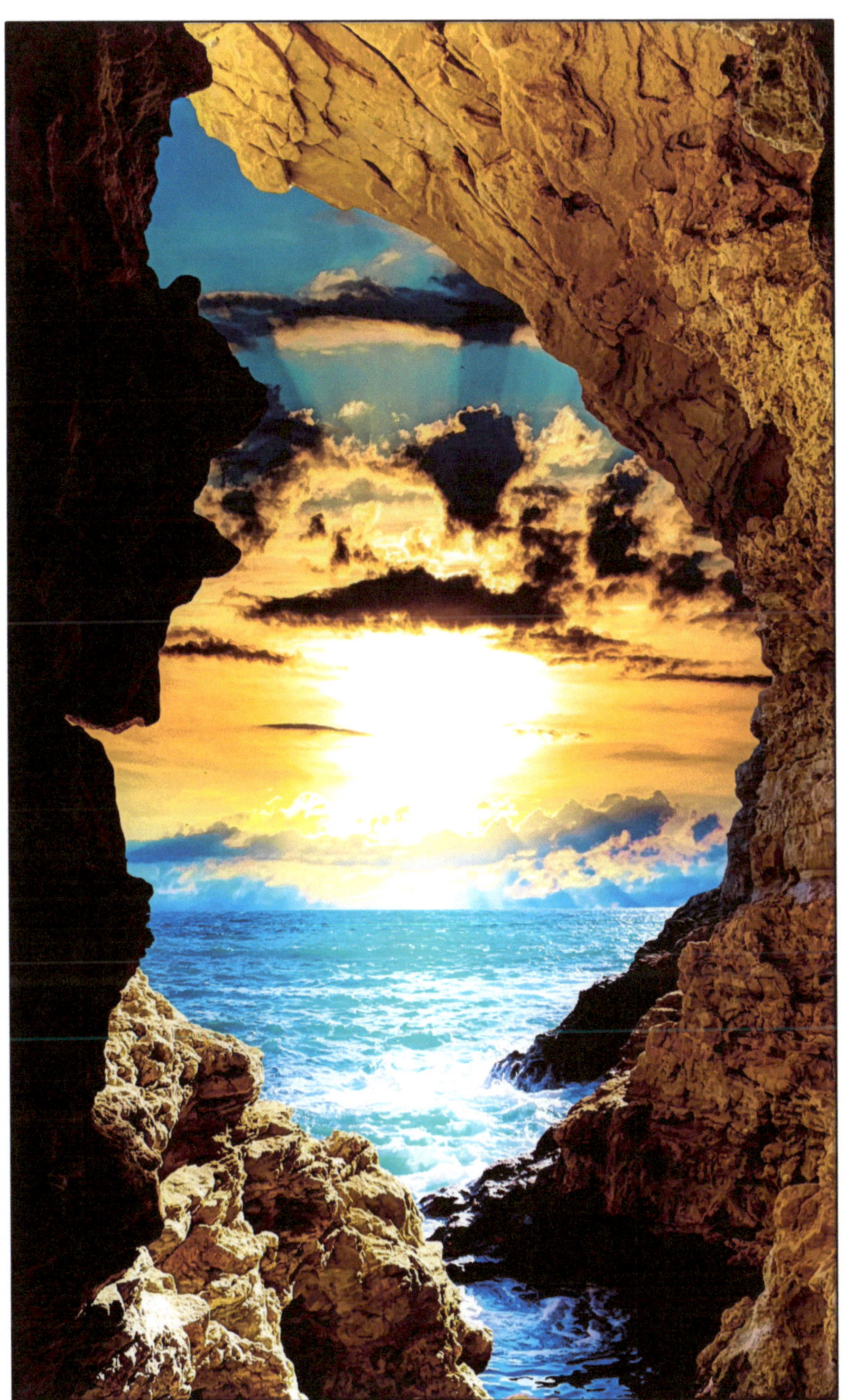

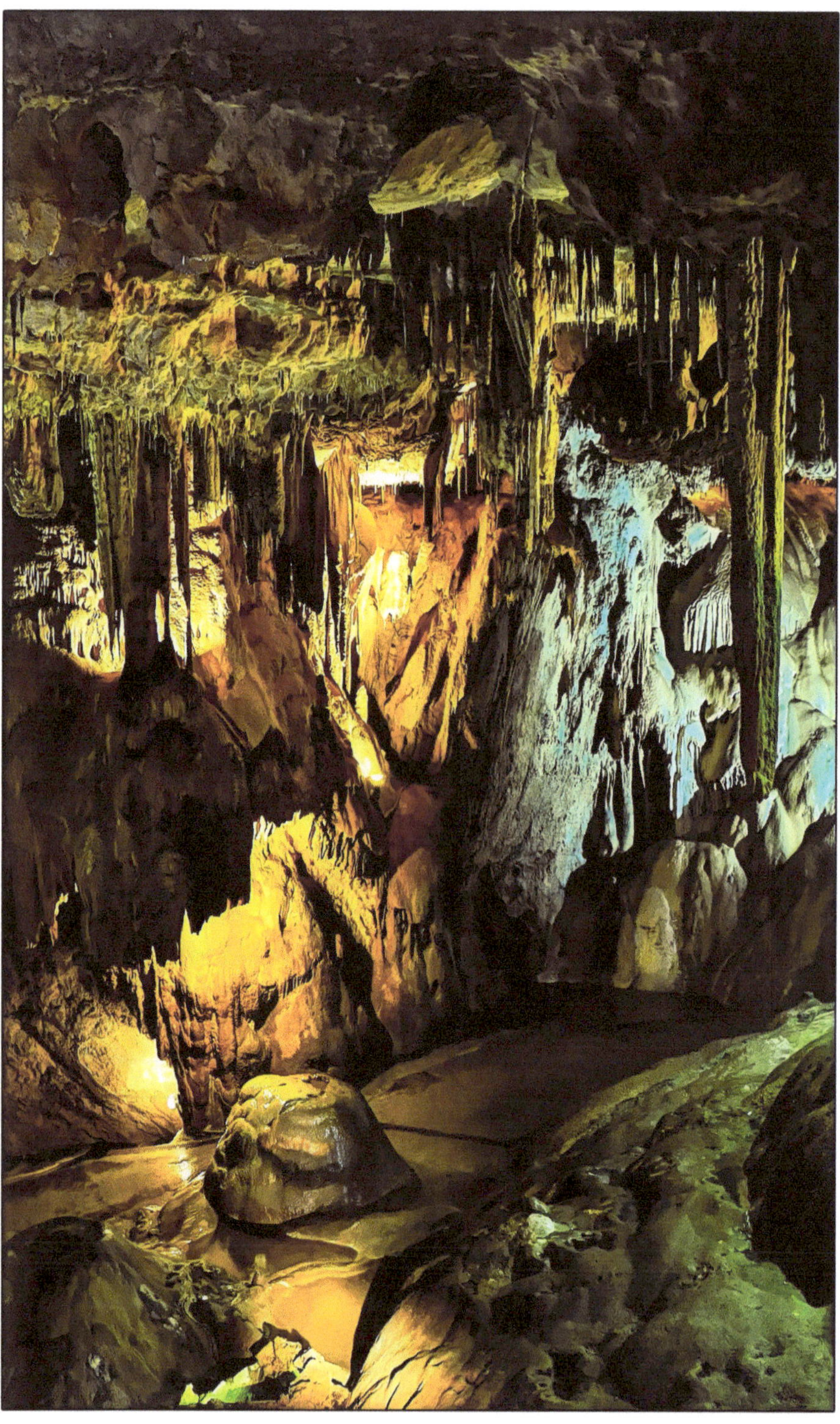

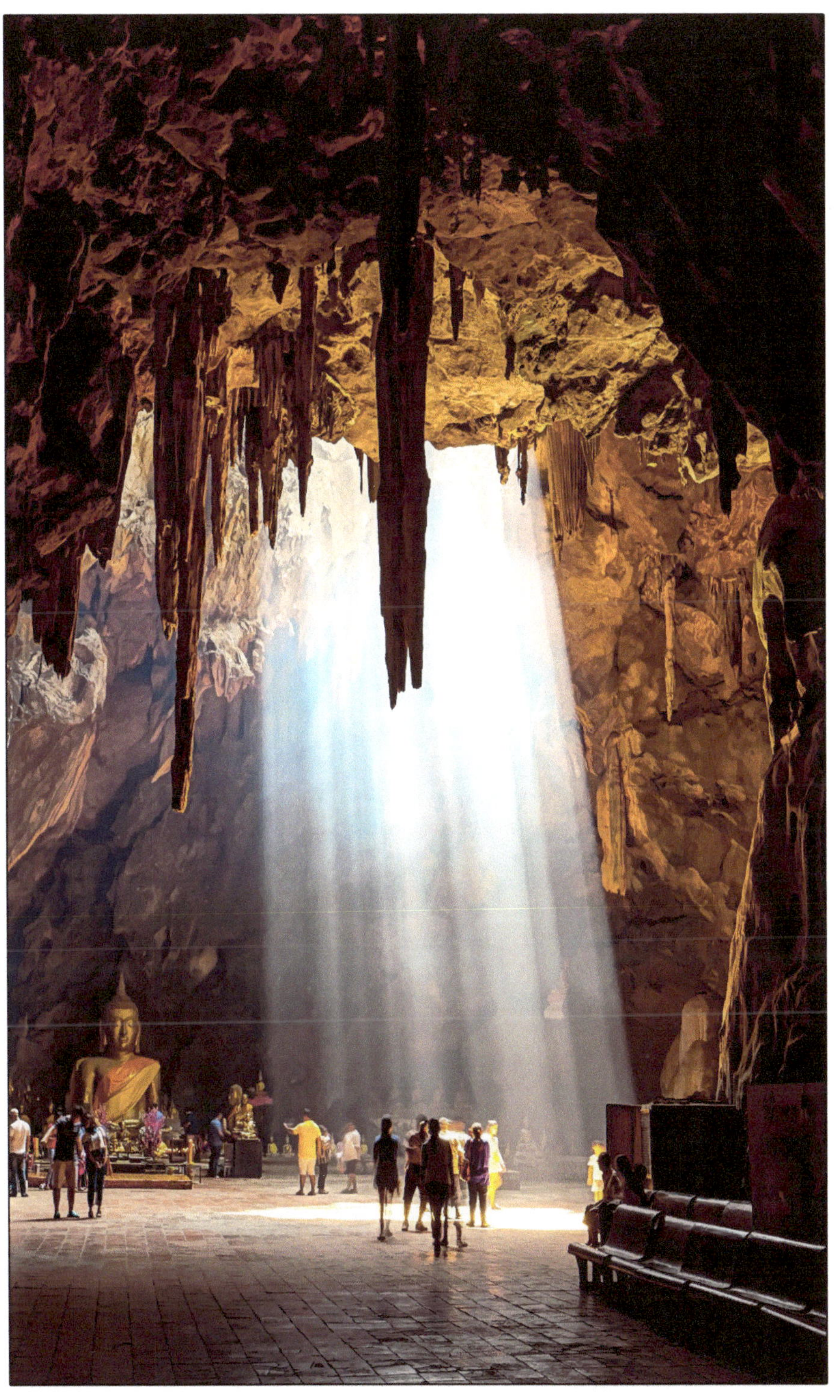

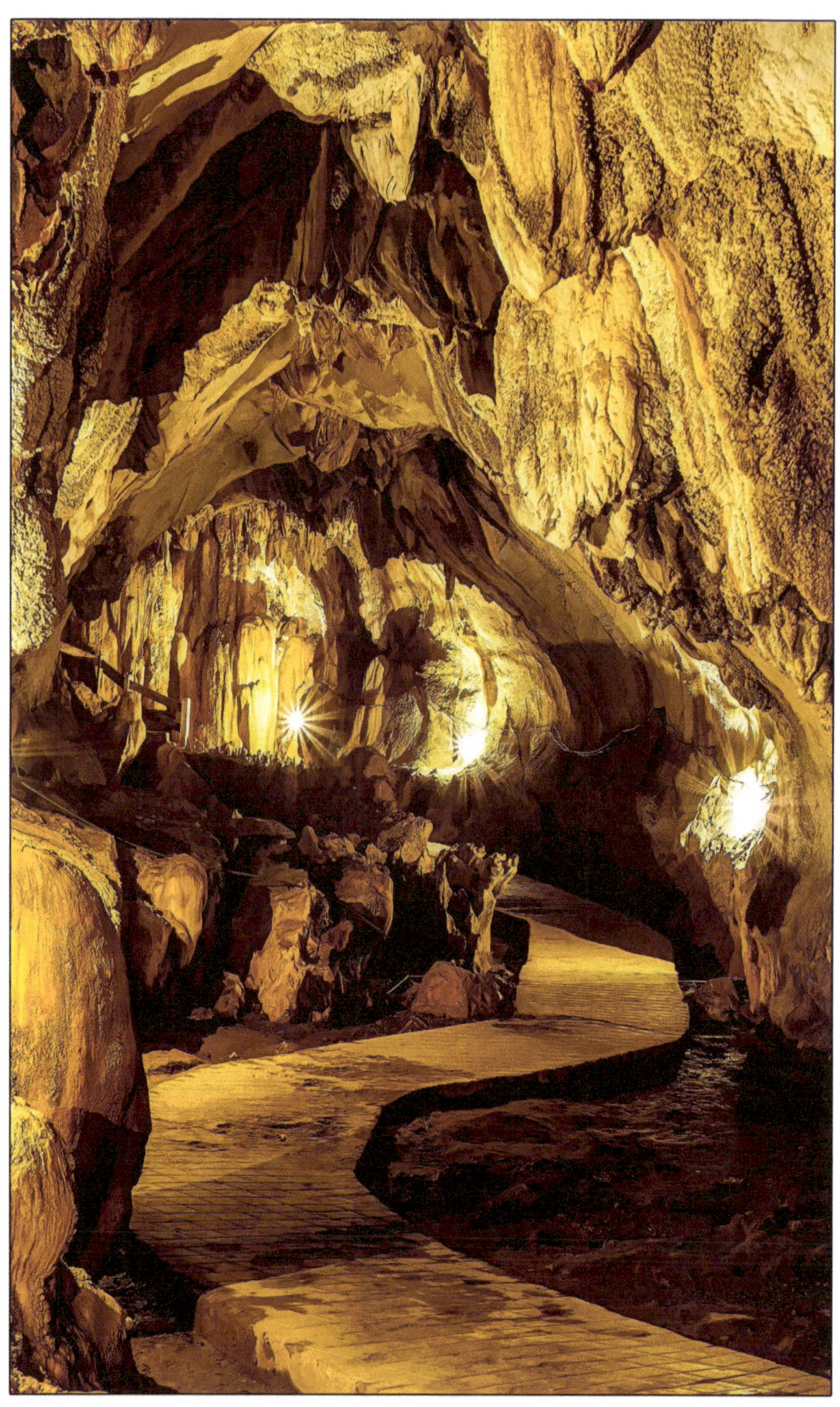

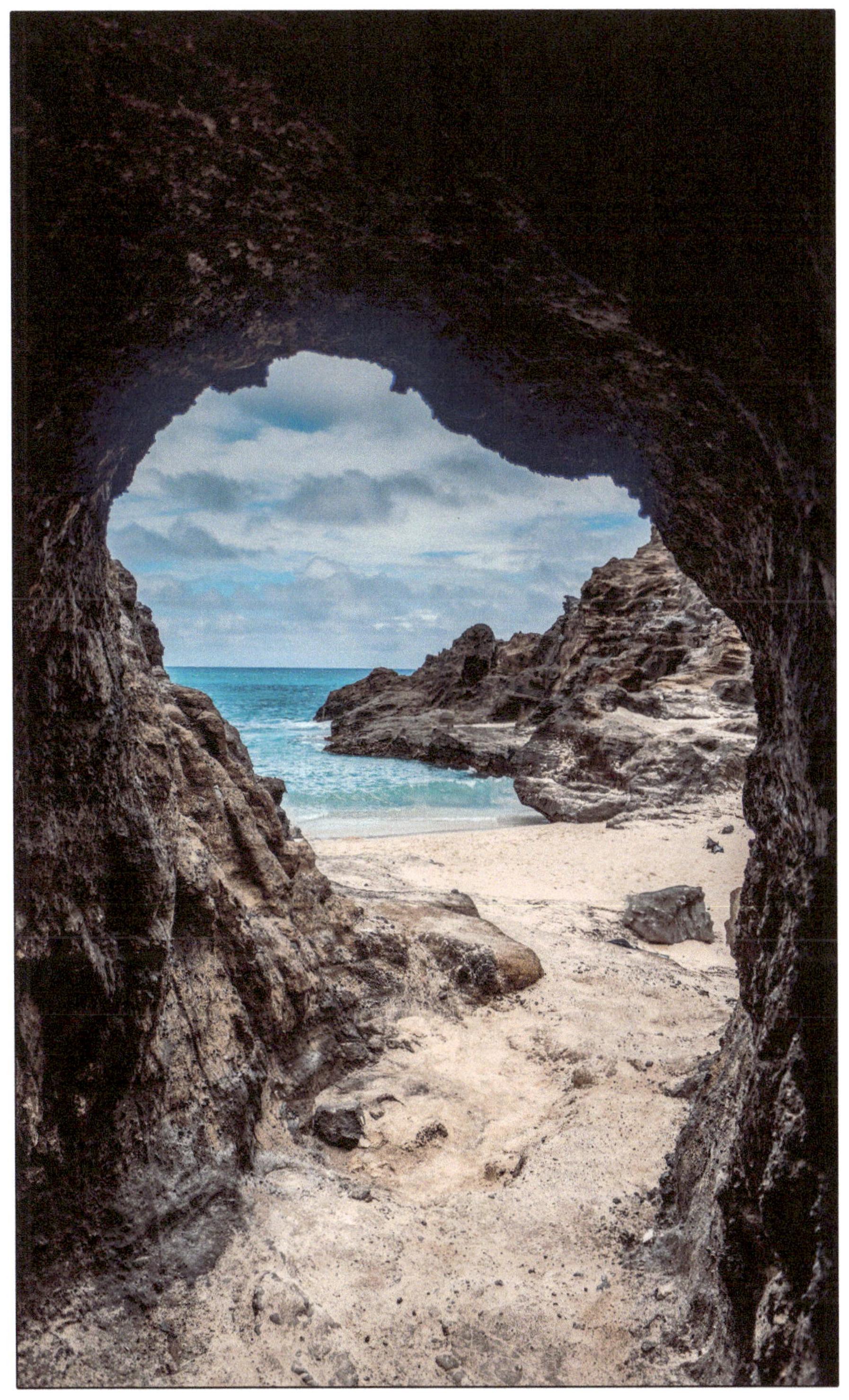

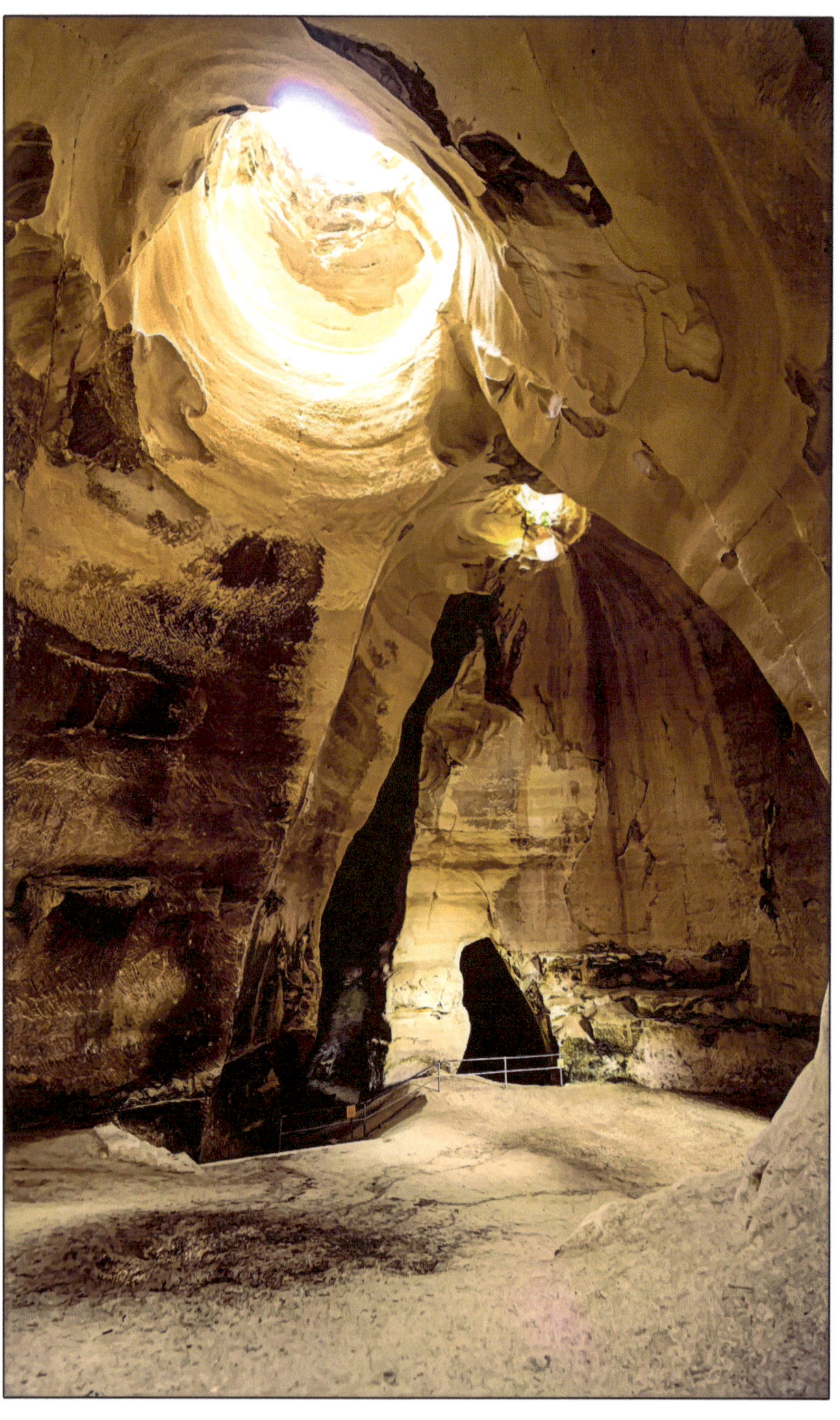

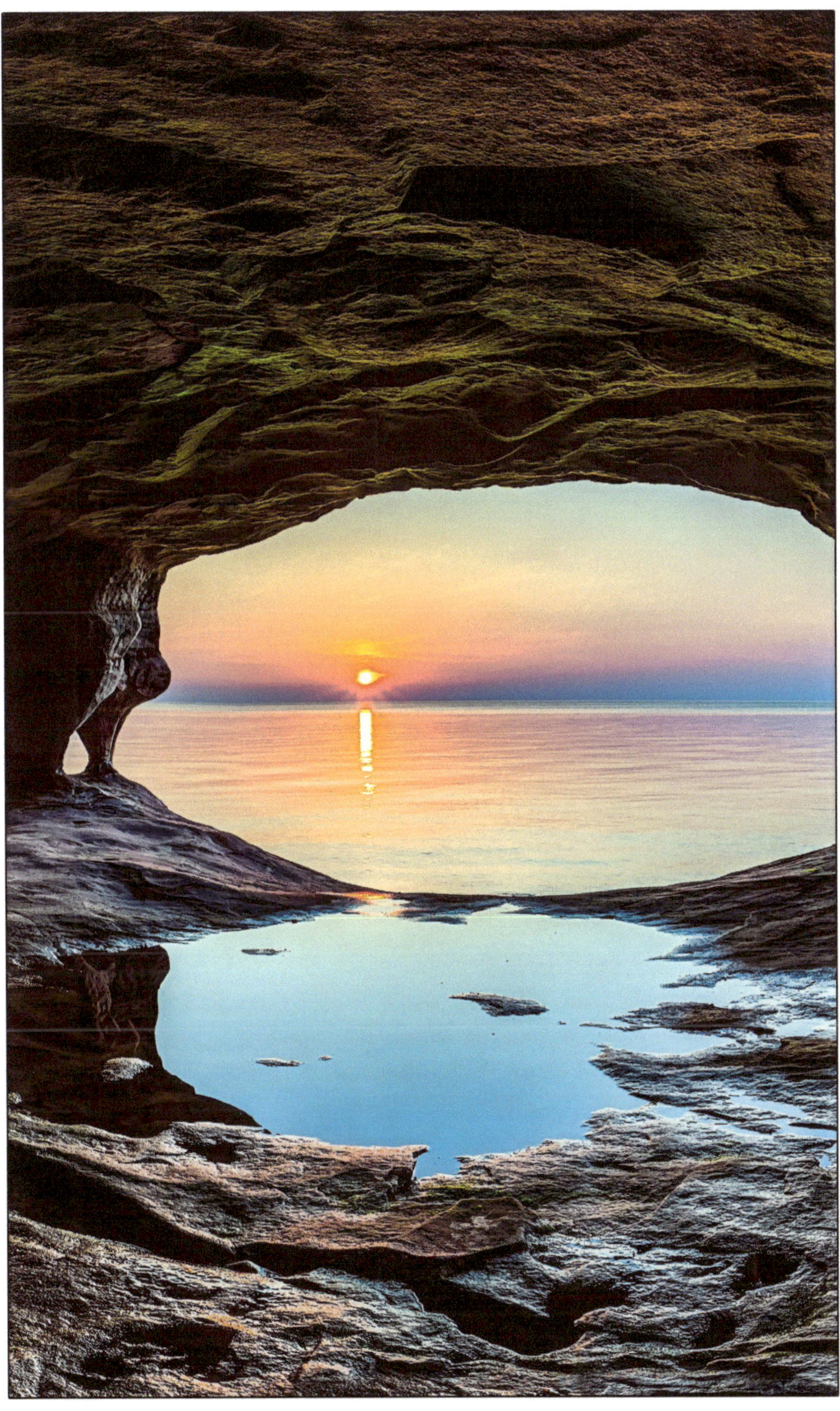

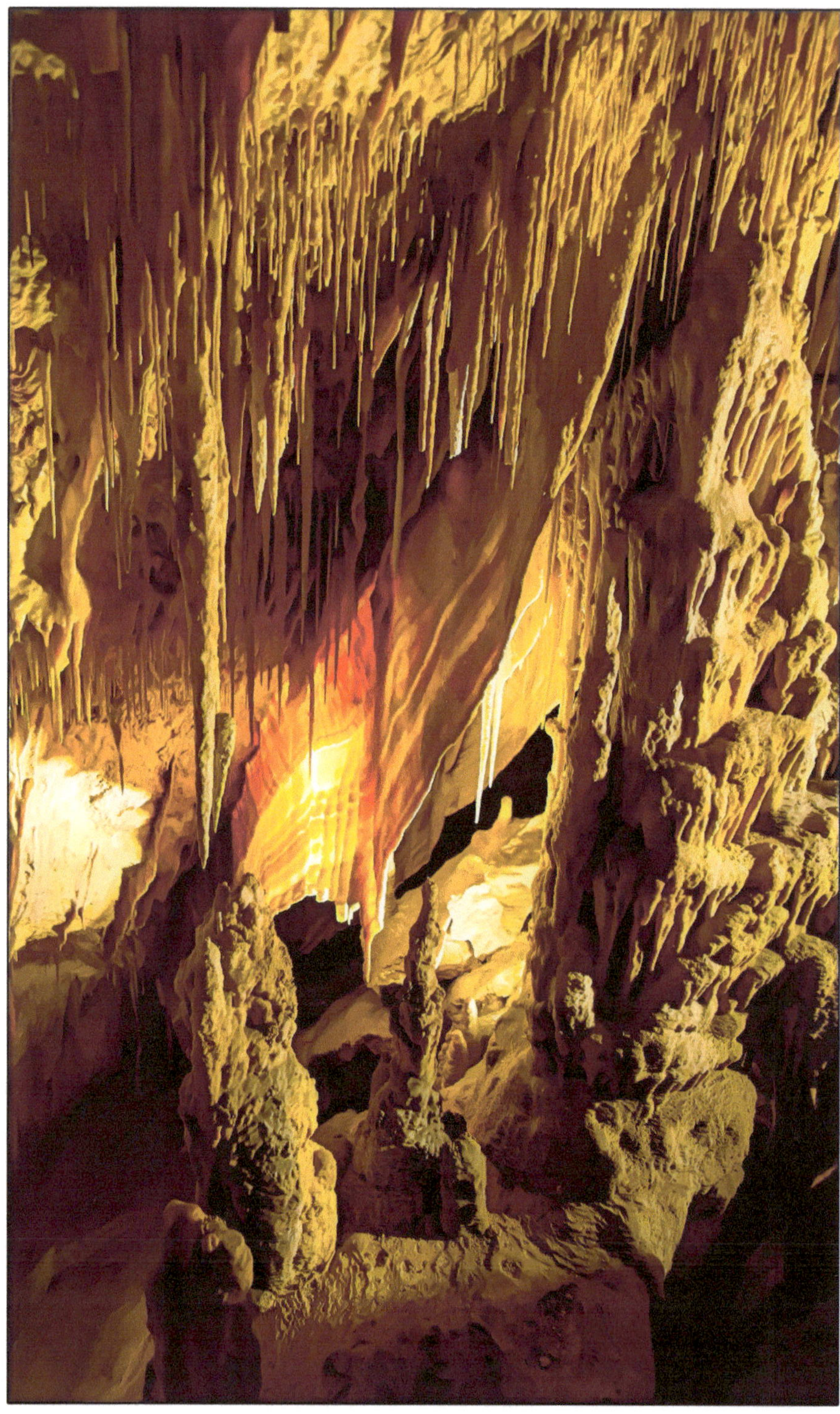

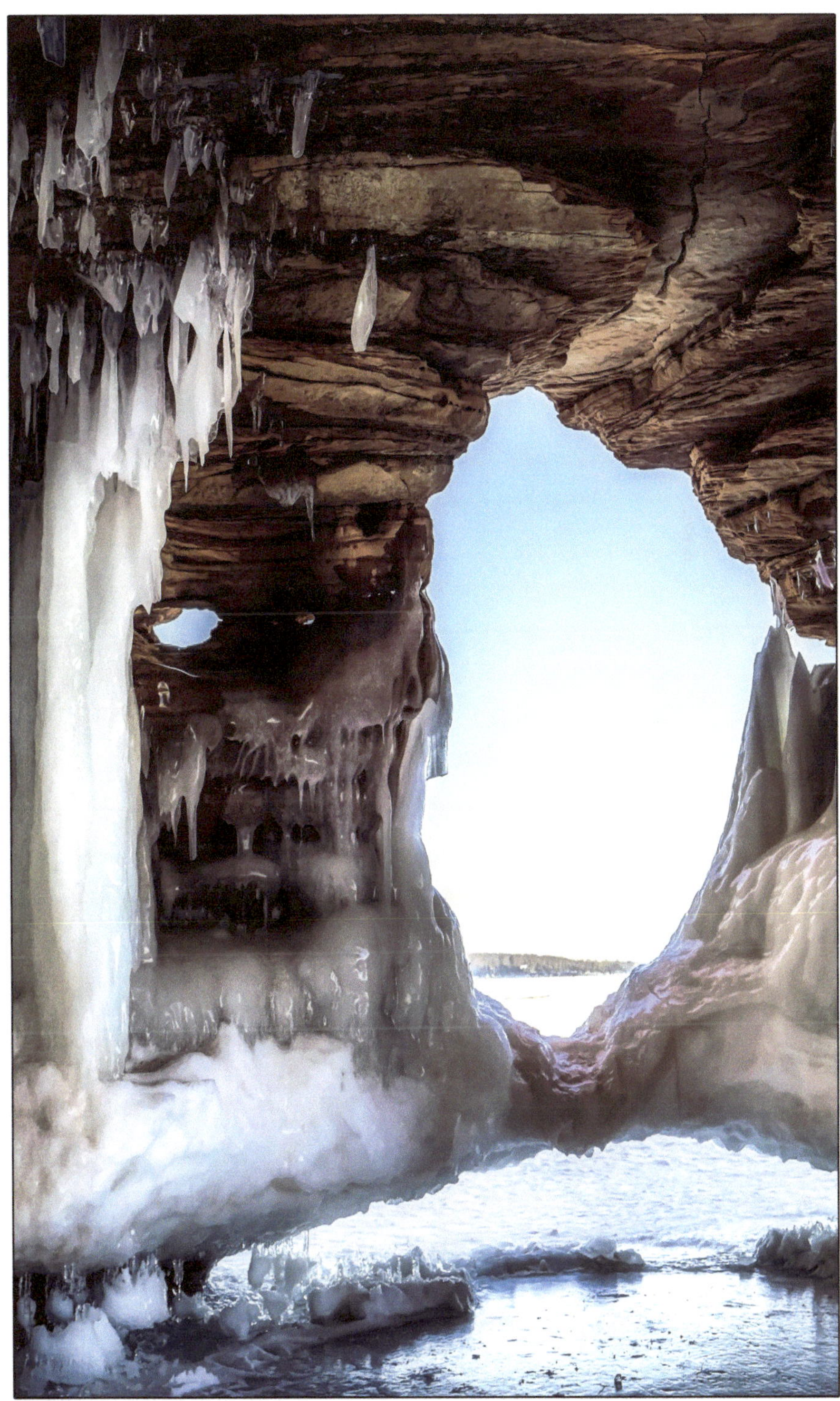

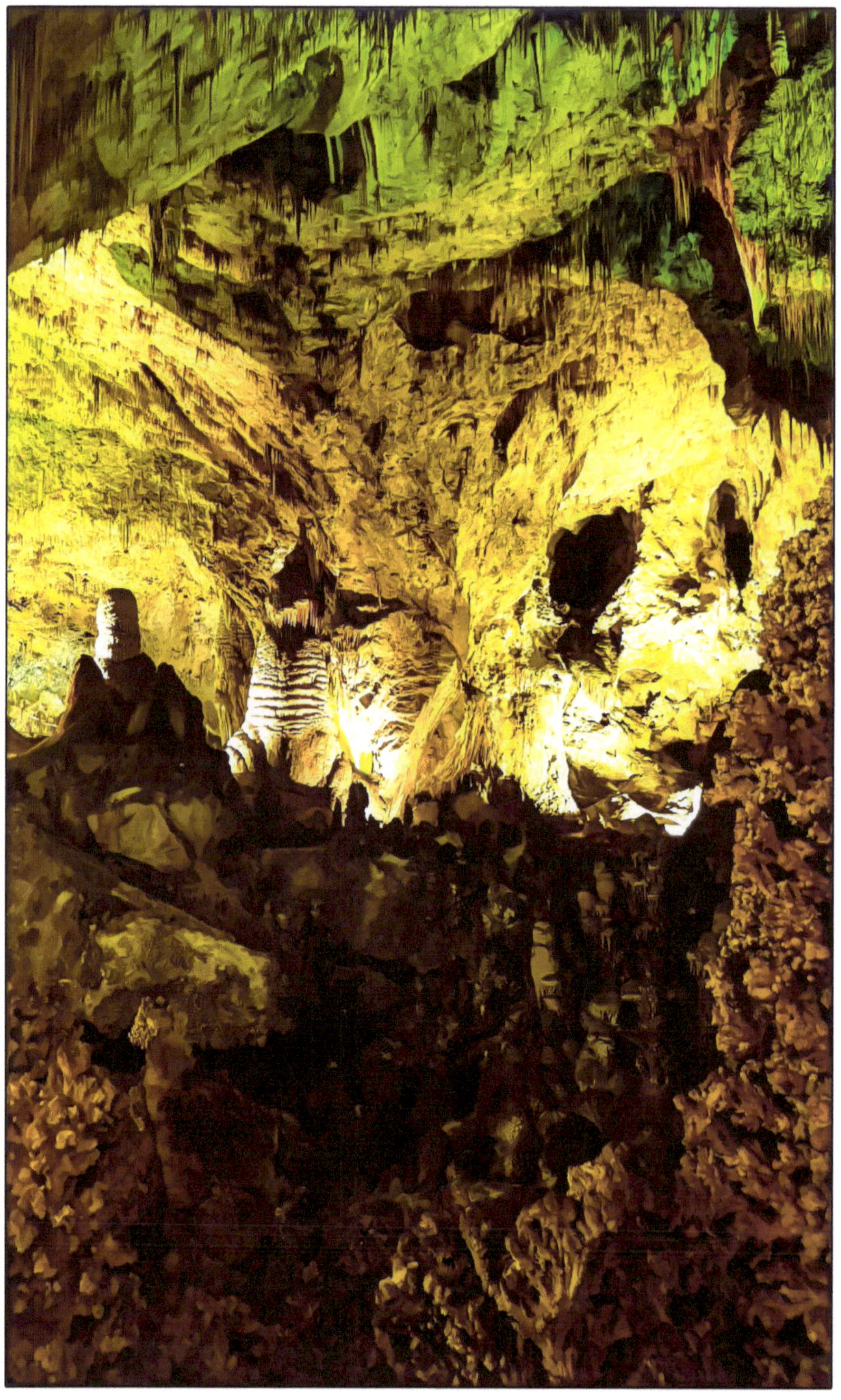

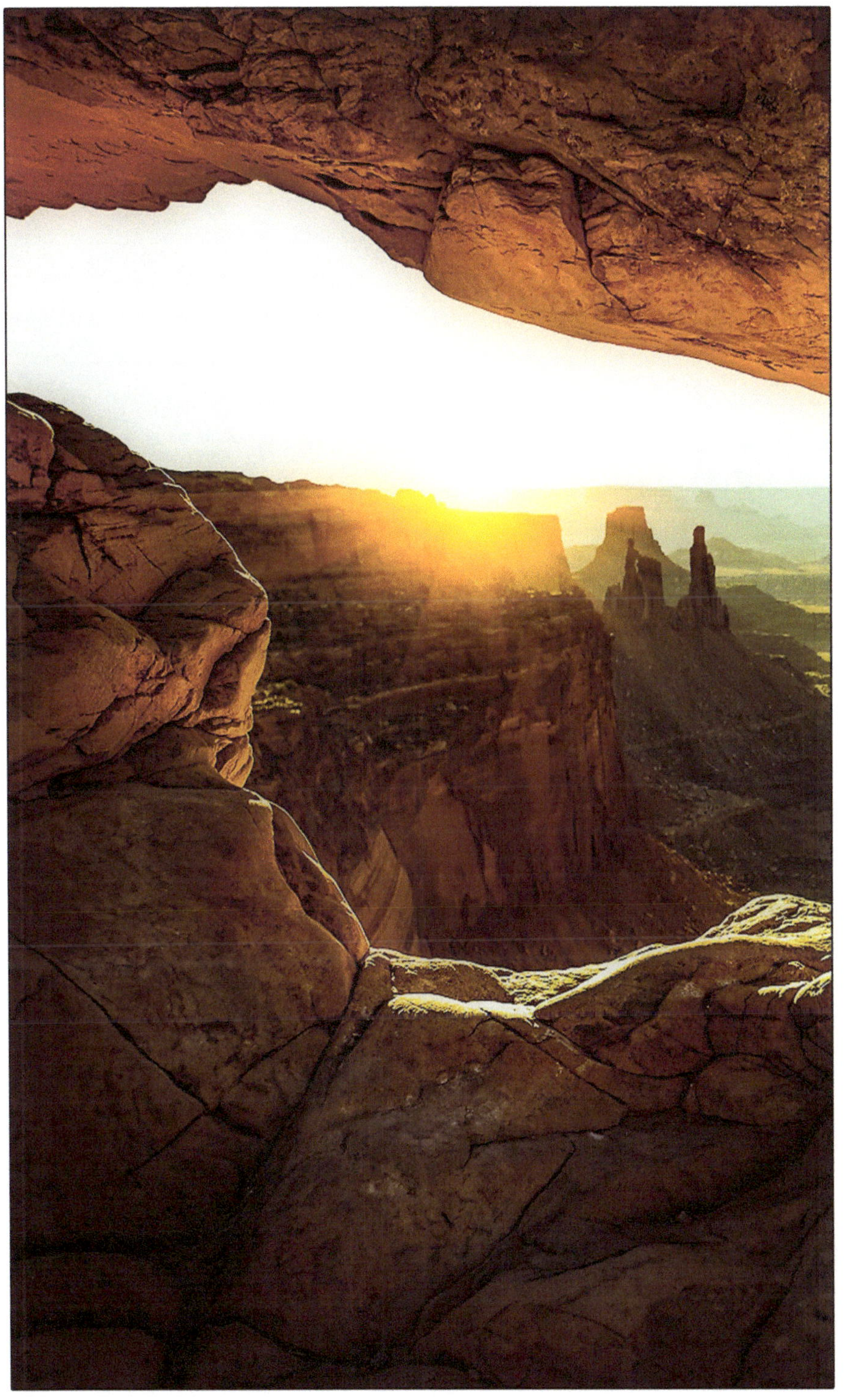

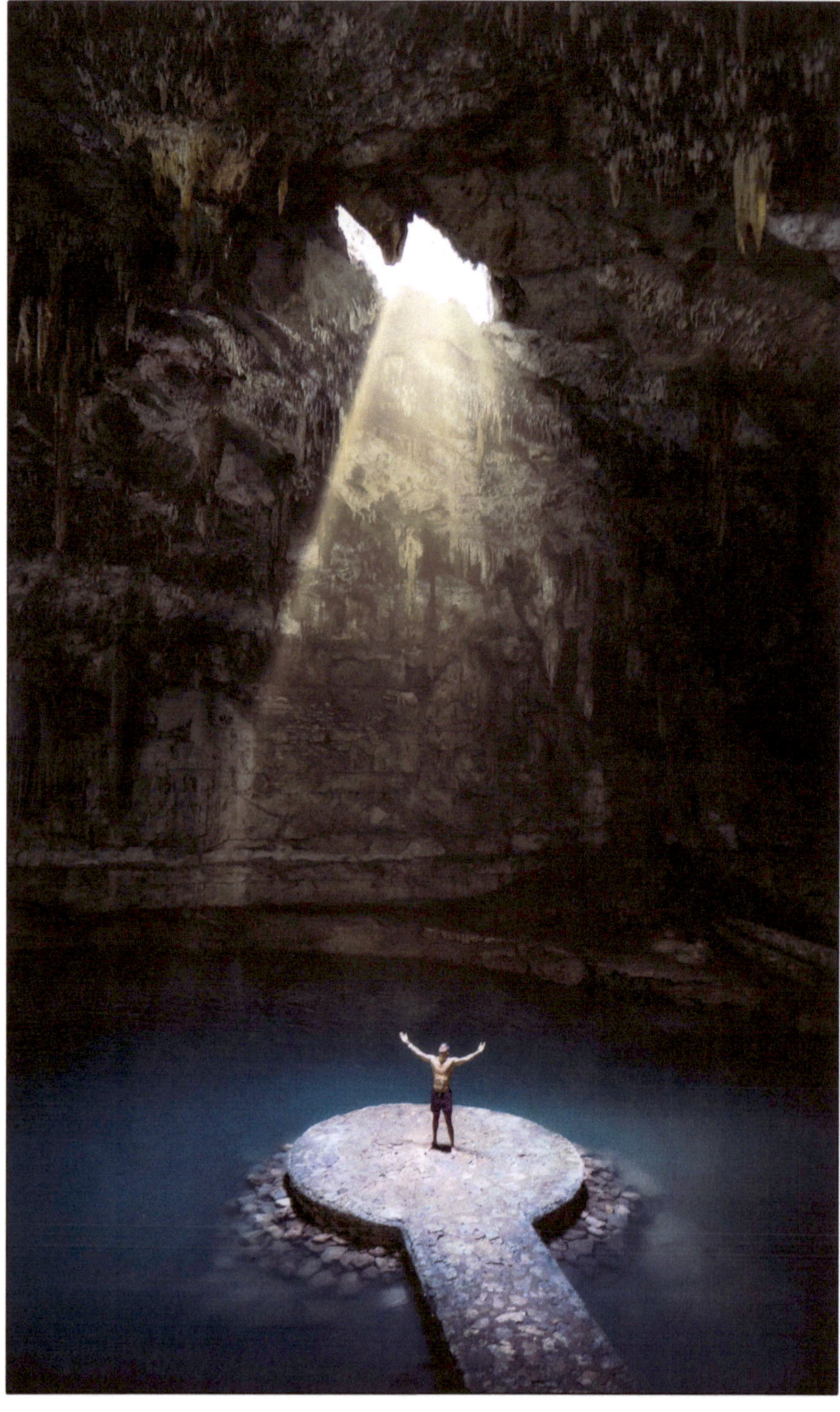

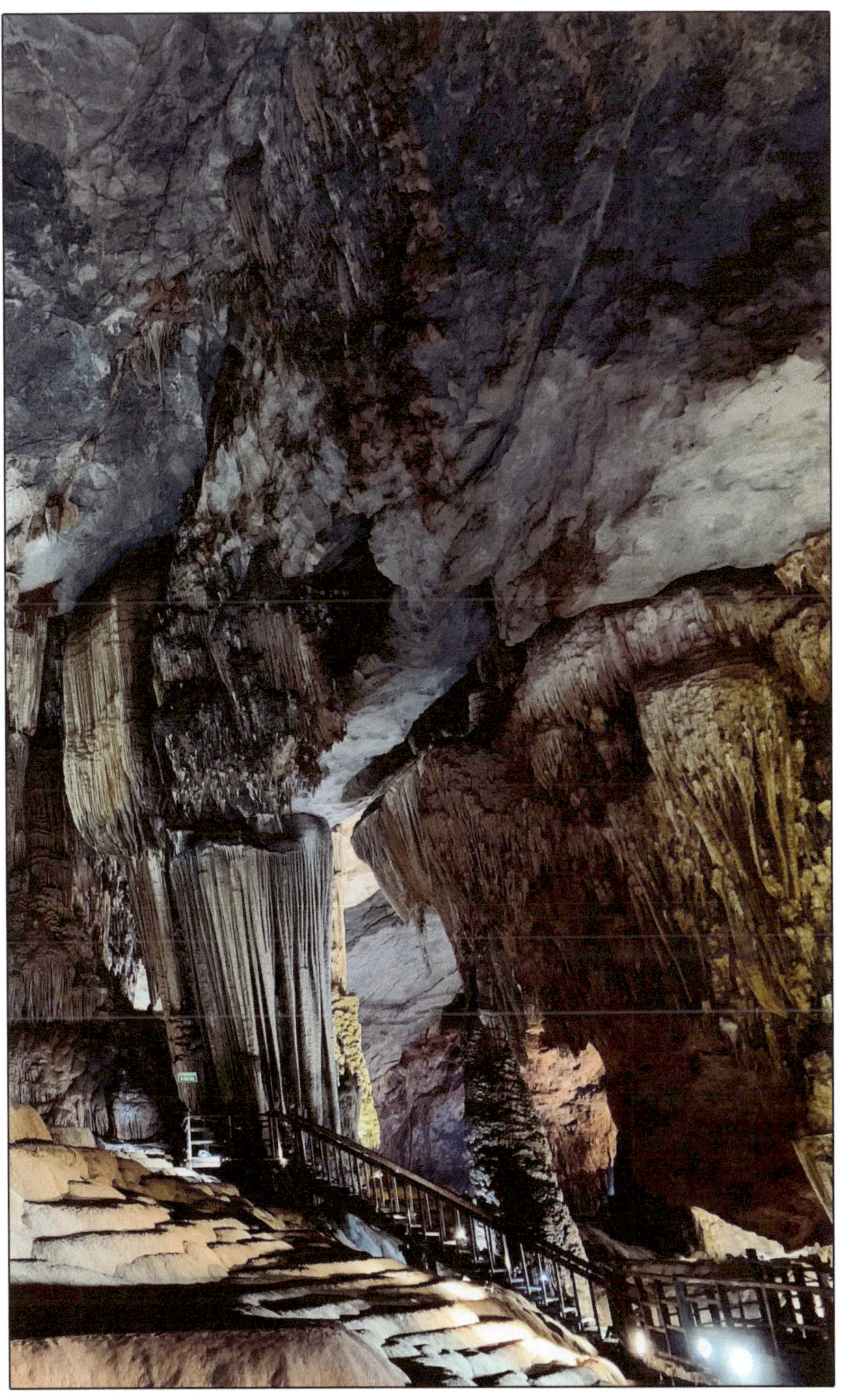

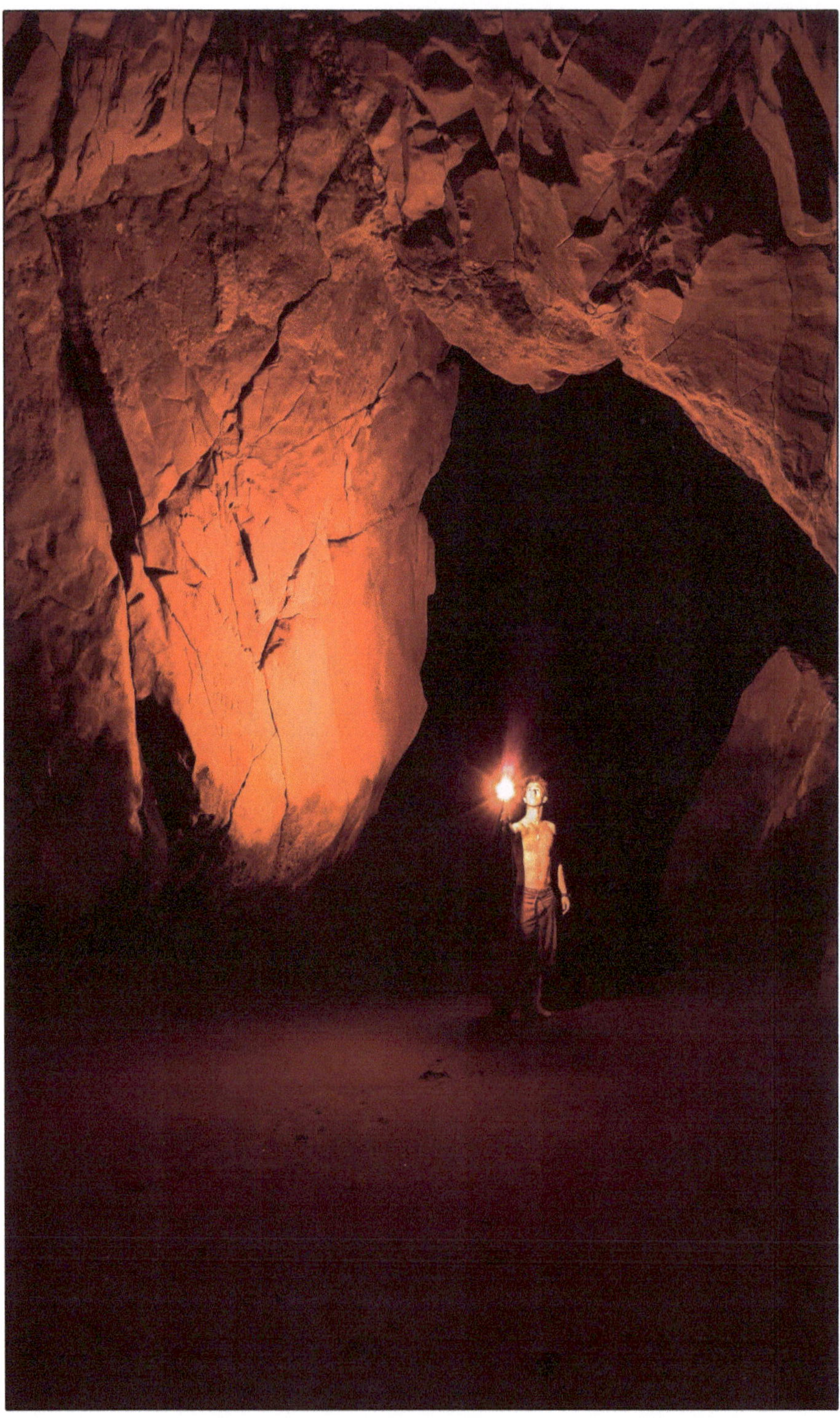

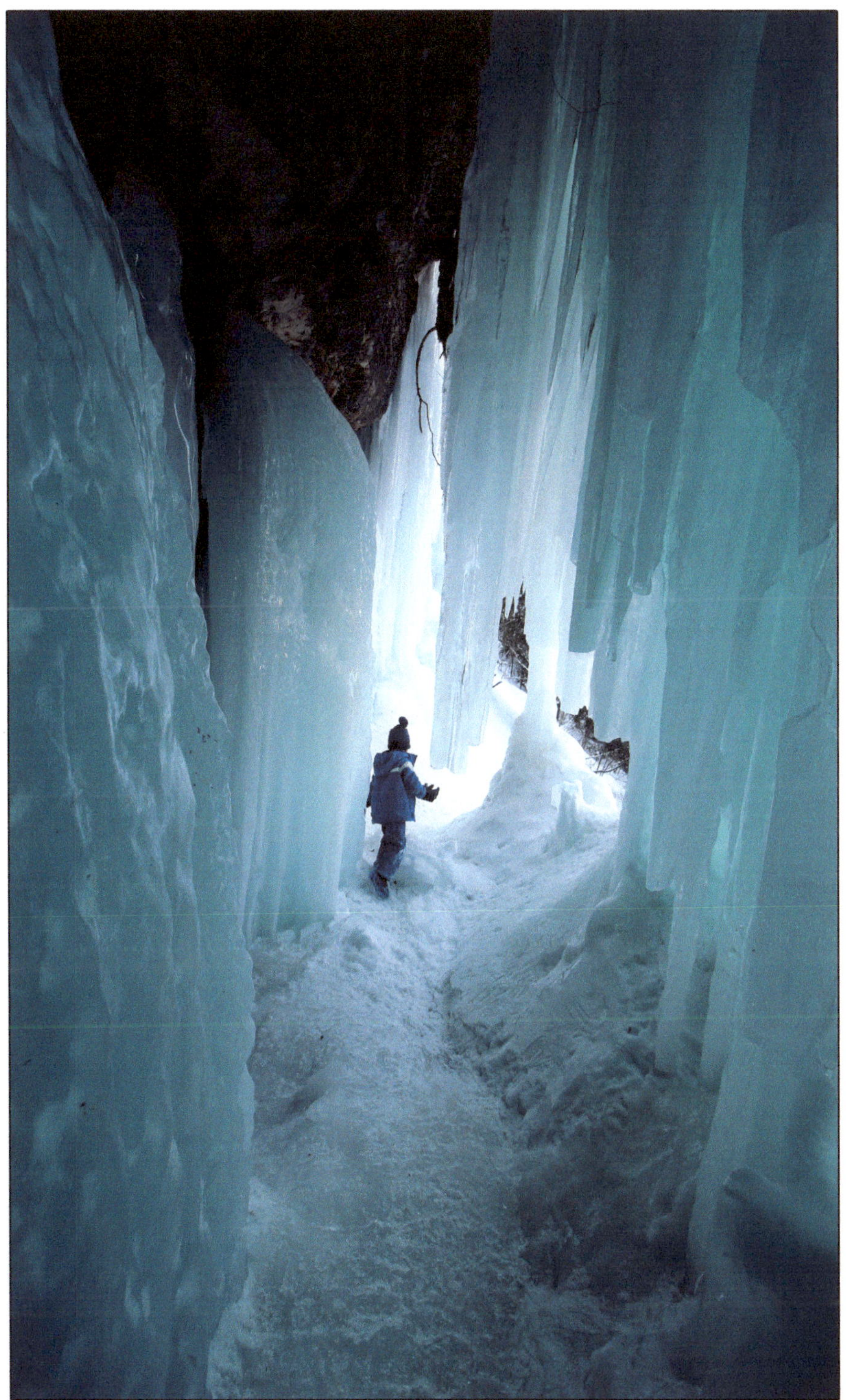

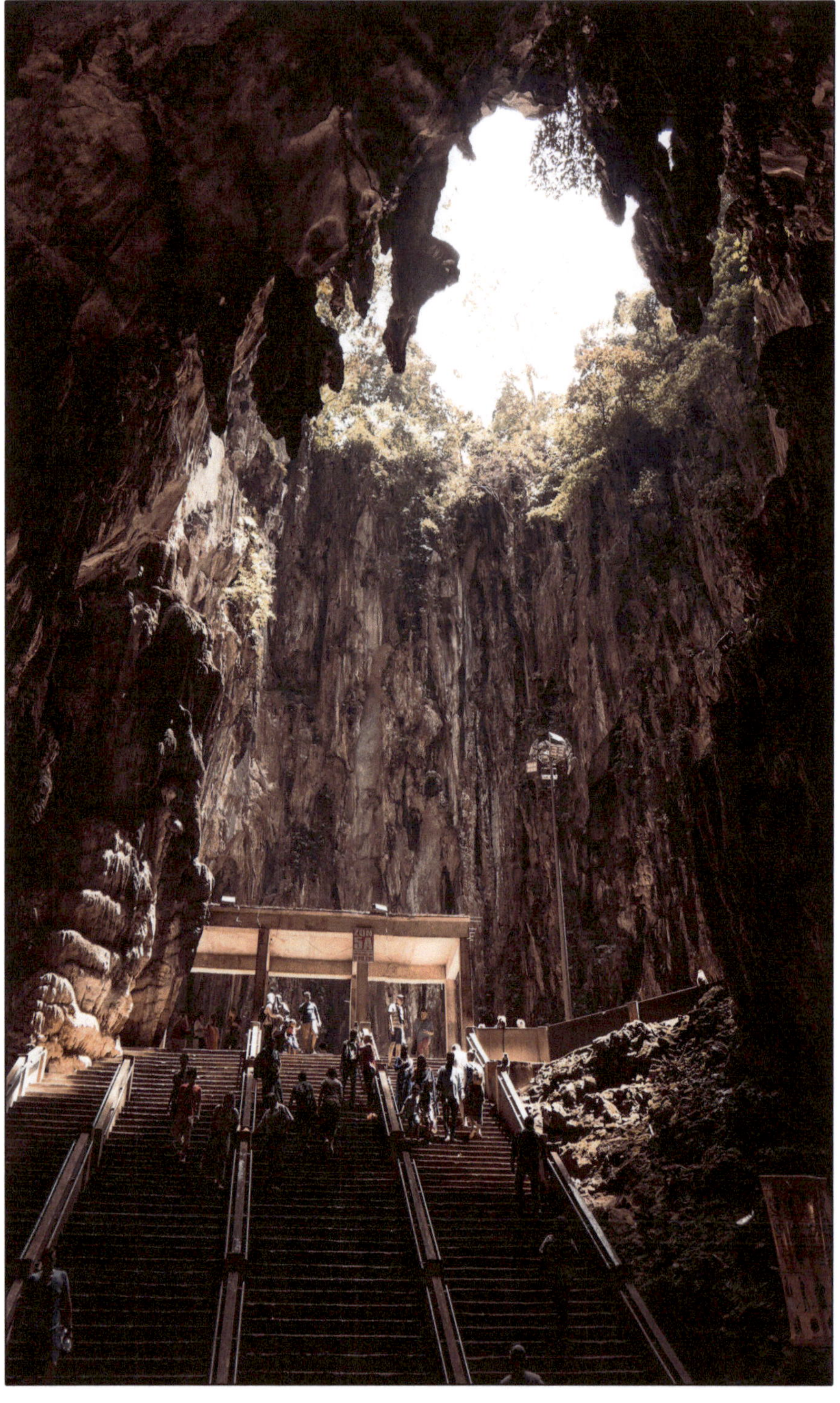

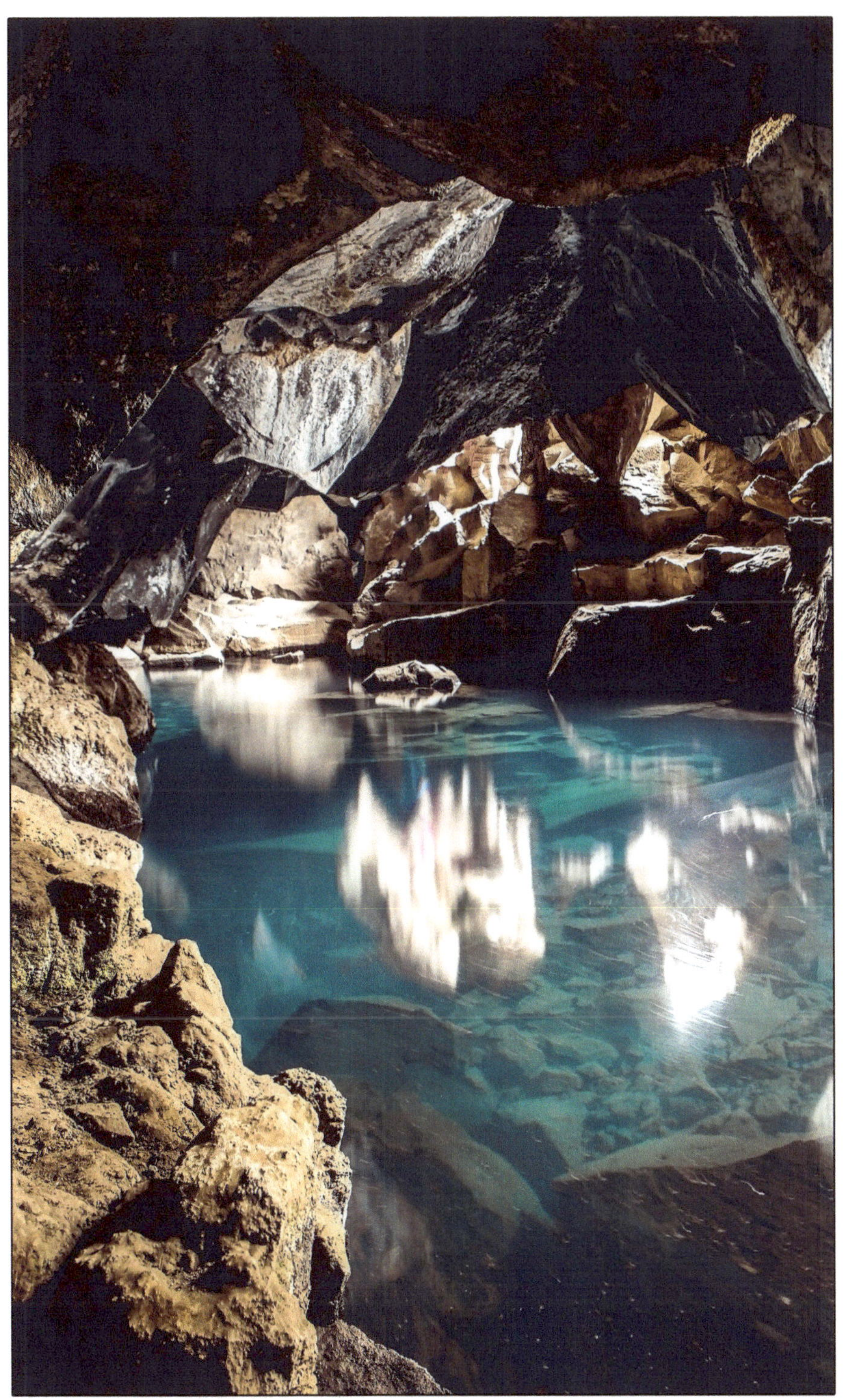